LETTERS
FROM
LEADERS

To

CHRIS

From

LETTERS
FROM
LEADERS

Personal Advice for Tomorrow's Leaders from
the World's Most Influential People

Compiled by HENRY O. DORMANN
Chairman and Editor in Chief, *LEADERS* Magazine

THE LYONS PRESS
Guilford, Connecticut
An Imprint of The Globe Pequot Press

The Lyons Press is an imprint of The Globe Pequot Press.

Text designed by Georgiana Goodwin

Library of Congress Cataloging-in-Publication Data is available on file.

ISBN 978-1-59921-501-3

Printed in the United States of America

10 9 8 7 6 5 4 3 2 1

CONTENTS

THE ROAD TO SUCCESS

The words in this book will inspire and enlighten
readers. These words will do additional good because
proceeds from the sales of the book are being donated
to fund scholarships for tomorrow's leaders in need
of financial support.

INTRODUCTION

All kings and queens, presidents, Nobel laureates, chairmen and chairwomen, CEOs, and world leaders have one thing in common: They want what they have achieved to be useful and to be handed over to a younger generation.

They want to be remembered for the good things they feel they've accomplished in industry, finance, philanthropy, public service, and education.

They may disagree on politics or business or lifestyle, but they all would like history to paint a positive picture of their legacy.

Some leave money, others leave inspiration. Many leave both. But all are anxious for young people to learn from their successes and even their failures.

One becomes a sage with age. But what good is a sage who is silent?

The leaders in these pages have "lived" and now offer their experiences as a treasure to ambitious and open minds—those who want to be something in life.

Here then are some words to the wise from a lot of wise leaders. Words to use if you agree or to discard if you don't, but one way or another, to take as your own, to help you get ahead in life, and to help you become one of those leaders in the future.

Why not!

Henry Dormann

—Henry Dormann, Chairman and Editor in Chief
LEADERS magazine

LEADING OFF WITH "THE GREATEST"

Muhammad Ali

Now suffering from an incurable illness, Muhammad Ali nevertheless wrote this letter himself, composing all the words and under great concentration signing the letter. "The Greatest" has given us advice straight from his heart: Never give up, try to have fun, connect with other people, and do what you believe is right.

———————

Still the most recognizable man on Earth, Muhammad Ali burst onto the scene as a gold-medal winner at the 1960 Rome Olympics. He was dubbed "Athlete of the Century" by *GQ* magazine, "Sportsman of the 20th Century" by *Sports Illustrated,* and "Sports Personality of the Century" by the BBC. Whether promoting tolerance and understanding, feeding the hungry, or reaching out to children in need, Ali is devoted to making the world a better place for all people. In 2005 he received the United States' Presidential Medal of Freedom.

THE GREATER THE OBSTACLE, THE MORE
GLORIOUS THE MOMENT OF SUCCESS

Dr. Martin Luther King, Jr. once said, *"The time is always right to do what is right."* I think most people would agree with that. The tricky part, of course, is knowing "what is right." I wouldn't try to tell others how to decide important matters, but I will share with you how I try to work them out.

I have always been interested in what is going on around me. I listened, observed, and read, taking the ideas and information that made sense to me and adapting and adopting them for my life. I worked hard and then worked some more, trying to be the best that I could possibly be at what I was doing. I learned that tough times are a part of our journey in this life, but that challenges make life interesting. Even though it can be painful and frightening at the time, the greater the obstacle, the more glorious the moment of success. I decided not to close the door of opportunity on myself just because I wasn't sure I could do something. Even when I didn't get all the way to my goal, I found that when I tried as hard as I could, I was much further along than I otherwise would have been. And I found that the journey itself was a great adventure.

It is also important to have fun. I enjoyed my life. No matter where I was or what I was doing, I took the positive from the experience and lived in the moment, connecting with the people around me—whoever they were. I tried to make people feel good about themselves and to make them laugh, if I could.

Most of all, I believed in God and the wisdom He has for what my life should be.

Using all of these lessons as my guiding principles, not how much money or power and control over others I could command, I made the decisions I believed in my heart at the time were right. I accepted the consequences of my choices. For me doing "what is right" is everything.

OPTIMISM/OVERCOMING CHALLENGES

Vahid Alaghband

CHAIRMAN, BALLI KLÖCKNER

Vahid Alaghband has become a success as a foreign national headquartered in London. Dealing worldwide, his company is one of the largest traders in minerals. He is an opportunity watcher who takes advantage of every good possibility. Here he discusses how optimism can be found in the face of adverse situations by approaching your problems from different angles and always making use of your basic value system.

Vahid Alaghband is the founder and chairman of Balli Klöckner, a leading steel and commodities group. He is also a member of the British Institute of Directors, Confederation of British Industry, World Economic Forum Davos; a patron of the British Museum; a founding member and patron of the Iran Heritage Foundation; a member of the Cornell University Council; and a member of the Advisory Board of the Pauline Foundation.

LOOK FOR THAT SILVER LINING

My thinking is that people should search for the silver lining in every cloud. So one might look at what one considers a disaster at ten o'clock in the morning as a potential opportunity by five o'clock in the afternoon. The challenge is to be able to move 180 degrees around the problem and look for that silver lining. In my life I've always become stronger coming out of adverse situations, because I've looked for that silver lining.

The other thing is that you have to be optimistic, for life is full of opportunities just there for the taking. It's much more fashionable sometimes to be pessimistic about things, but, in every challenge, every problem, there's a solution and an opportunity.

I don't know of any easy ways to make money or succeed in life. Most of the people I know are successful, and most of them are much more successful than I am. They do it by hard work, having the right ideas, and going by the book. I think if we go back to some of the basic values that make the current generation of industrial and financial leaders great, the next generation will have use of those values, have better tools, and bring about a future that's going to be more successful than the past.

T. Boone Pickens

CHAIRMAN OF THE BOARD AND CHIEF EXECUTIVE OFFICER, BP CAPITAL

A Texas dynamo even as he grows older, T. Boone Pickens has been correct in his judgment in the future of oil, gas, and energy—and he's made a lot of money being correct. He describes in his letter the importance of perseverance, even in the face of daunting challenges.

T. Boone Pickens built the largest independent oil company in the United States and flourished as an entrepreneur after leaving it. Among his lengthy accolades, *Financial World* named him "CEO of the Decade" in 1989 and the *Oil & Gas Journal* listed him as one of the "100 Most Influential People of the Petroleum Century." During the span of his career, Pickens has made hundreds of millions of dollars—for others as well as himself—and he isn't timid about spreading it around. The breadth of his philanthropy—more than $600 million— includes medical research, athletics, and academic projects.

TO BE UP AGAINST THE WALL

Number one: You have to stay in there and keep pitching. Someone once said to me, "Pickens, you just like to get your back against the wall to demonstrate that you can get off the wall." Of course I don't like it, but I don't find it all that uncomfortable to be up against the wall. I always know I'll pull it out.

Don't let anything overcome you. In the 1990s, I had a bout with depression. I never thought it would happen to me, but it did. But I wasn't depressed for very long. I was able to overcome it, and without any reoccurrence. I cleared up some things in my life. If I couldn't fix something, I just moved on. I don't spend a lot of time working on things I can't fix.

Young people have to have self-confidence, especially if they get into a spot that requires a lot of fortitude to overcome. I've always had a lot of self-confidence.

Peter G. Peterson

SENIOR CHAIRMAN, THE BLACKSTONE GROUP

Former chairman of Lehman Brothers and one of the founders of the Blackstone Group, Peter G. Peterson semiretired as a multi, multi-billionaire, and he's using his money in a foundation he created to give back to the public in the form of scholarships. Through his family story, Peterson reveals to us the values and lessons that have led him to success.

Peter G. Peterson is senior chairman and cofounder of the Blackstone Group, a private investment banking company. He is chairman of the Council on Foreign Relations, founding chairman of the Institute for International Economics (Washington, D.C.), and founding president of the Concord Coalition, a citizen's group dedicated to building a constituency of fiscal responsibility.

Prior to founding Blackstone, Peterson was chairman and chief executive officer of Lehman Brothers and later chairman and chief executive officer of Lehman Brothers, Kuhn, Loeb Inc. He also served as U. S. Secretary of Commerce.

AN EXUBERANT CONFIDENCE IN THE FUTURE

I am the firstborn son of Greek immigrants. In today's world of fragile and failing role models, their example is as indelible as it is inspiring.

My father, George Petropoulos, and my mother, Venetia Pavlopoulos, each single and alone, came to America in their teens with nothing more than third-grade educations from schools in remote Greek farm villages. They were fearful, but opportunities in their homeland were meager and the promise of America filled them with hope and confidence. After all, the United States of America was the land of limitless frontiers, the land where dreams came true.

Like many other young men, George Petropoulos headed west soon after his arrival in 1912. And like so many immigrants, then and now, he took whatever work a recent immigrant speaking a foreign tongue could find. He made his way to Nebraska, where he joined his older brother Nick, who was working for the Union Pacific Railroad. Because the foreman had trouble pronouncing the family name, Nick changed Petropoulos (which means "son of Peter") to Peterson. My father also took the new name, so I was born a Peterson. Years later he told me he was sorry he had changed our name. In his always clear but often broken English, here is how he put it: "I wouldn't want anyone to think we weren't proud of 'our race.'"

He worked long, sweltering hours at a menial job no one else wanted—washing dishes in a steaming caboose kitchen. Although he didn't earn much, he saved most of what he earned. He borrowed as little as possible— and even then, only to invest in a better future for his family. "My son," he used to say, "if we spend a little less and save a little more today, we will all have a lot tomorrow."

Slowly but steadily my father's savings accumulated and before long were transmuted into the inevitable Greek diner, the Central Café in Kearney, Nebraska. It was an establishment distinguished not only for its cuisine but for the fact that for a full quarter century it stayed open twenty-four hours a day, seven days a week, 365 days a year. And for many—too many—of those hours, days, weeks, and years, my father was on his feet in that restaurant, varicose veins and all.

As a child during the Great Depression, I recall watching with a mixture of pride and edginess as my father offered food (often in return for simple chores) to any jobless, out-of-luck soul who approached the back door of the Central Café. Throughout his working life he shared what fortune he had with his family, his community, and with the rural community he left behind in Greece. He bought homes for sisters and brothers still living there and paid for so many municipal improvements in Vahlia that the village's main street is now called Petropoulos Street. In 1963 King Paul awarded him the First Gold Medal in recognition of his philanthropy.

True to his Mediterranean heritage, my father was an emotional man. "God Bless America," the only American song he could sing, never failed to produce patriotic tears. His America was about an exuberant confidence in the future that withstood even the economic collapse and fearful headlines of the 1930s. His America was also about faith in our freedoms and in equality of opportunity. It was a faith that withstood even the Ku Klux Klan when it picketed his restaurant with signs saying, "Don't eat with the Greek." "Those aren't real Americans," he told me. After all, *he* was a proud member of the Elks. His Sunday poker game at the Elks Club—the highlight of his week—sealed his acceptance by the community and demonstrated that, in those days, much of what fell into the American melting pot actually melted.

Many years later, when I informed him that President Nixon had invited me to join the White House, my father did not hesitate for a second. "You have no choice," he said. "It is your duty to serve *our* country." Before long he was known to greet newcomers with an unusual salutation: "Good morning. My son is the first and only Greek cabinet officer in the United States Government." No doubt I would have winced had I been present, and no doubt he would not have cared. My father's pride in any and all of the achievements of his family was irrepressible. No other pleasure was comparable.

And the role model of my father has become part of my very being. Without it, I don't think that I could have achieved whatever success I have enjoyed.

E. Marie McKee

Steuben Glass works of art are traditionally what presidents of the United States give to visiting heads of state, and E. Marie McKee not only oversees this aspect of the nation's most prestigious crystal company but also the glass museum in Corning, New York, which houses the country's most valuable collection of prize art crystal and other glass extravaganzas. McKee explains in her letter that exploration, optimum effort, and the willingness to ask questions can drive us to success.

E. Marie McKee has been a key figure at Corning Incorporated in designing and implementing human resource strategies, business processes, and organization change efforts. In 1998, McKee was named chairman of Steuben and president of the Corning Museum of Glass. Steuben Glass has won worldwide acclaim by virtue of its excellent design, material, and craftsmanship.

WHEN A DOOR CLOSES, ANOTHER OPENS

Understand your strengths and give yourself permission and time to explore options for your future. You set your own limits when you don't expose yourself to new ideas, new people, and new challenges. You will find things that you are good at doing and that significantly interest you. Your passion will emerge through this exploration.

As difficulties arise, be assured that as long as you try your best—truly your best—it is all that is or can be expected of you. Asking for help is not a sign of weakness but rather the action required to achieve a goal. And learn from your mistakes, incorporate the learning, and move forward.

And always, always remember, life is a journey which goes by more quickly each year.

Life has many interesting and intriguing twists and turns. I am a believer in the idea that when a door closes, another opens. Head high, smile on your face, walk through that open door.

TO BE OR NOT TO BE

Walter Cronkite

JOURNALIST

Probably the most respected journalist for generations, Walter Cronkite is also a kind, generous, and very human gentleman. Although he's written many books, his inside stories of what some of the famous people in the world he encountered were really like would make a fabulous best seller, but he vows never to put those personal anecdotes in writing. Yet in his letter he gives us an anecdote about himself to illustrate the point that, as he says, "There are no shortcuts to perfection."

A pioneer broadcaster who began his distinguished career as a wire service reporter, Walter Cronkite joined CBS in 1950 as a television correspondent, was named anchor of the *CBS Evening News* in 1962, and the following year launched network television's first thirty-minute newscast. He reported on the pivotal stories of the era—the assassination of John F. Kennedy, the battles over civil rights, the Vietnam War, the Apollo moon landings, and the Watergate scandal. Cronkite stepped down from the anchor desk at CBS News in 1981. He has received journalism's and television's highest awards.

BE PREPARED

The challenges in my life scarcely can compare with those of the world leaders also represented here.

Mine were those of a newspaper reporter and broadcaster. The fate of nations or of great corporations hardly hung on how I confronted them. The decisions I made affected, for the most part, only me—my professional future or perhaps, in the stress of wartime, my survival.

Early in my broadcast career I was hired to broadcast University of Oklahoma football games. To ease the formidable task of identifying all the players on both teams, I devised an electric board by which spotters from the opposing teams would, by simply pressing a button, identify for me the names of those involved in each of the plays.

With utmost confidence in my labor-saving device, I took my seat in the broadcast booth with the top executives of the broadcast station and our sponsors there to wish me well in an enterprise in which they had risked much on this neophyte football announcer.

Their confidence in me and my confidence in myself collapsed with the first play of the game. My spotters made mistakes as they punched the identifying buttons on my electric board. The nature of their mistakes ran the gamut of all the possibilities for error. The broadcast was a disaster.

The station owners and the sponsors were kinder than I deserved. They gave me another chance on the basis of my plan for rehabilitation.

I recruited as my spotter to punch the buttons on my electric machine, another station employee. He and I memorized the names and jersey numbers, ages, physical characteristics, and hometowns of every one of the thirty or forty members of every squad of every university we played—and, of course, the same for OU.

We spent three or four hours a day drilling our memories. One of us would call out a single fact about each player—name or number. The other had to fill in all the details of his football biography.

It was grueling, unglamorous work that began on Monday and went right up to game time the following Saturday. We missed a lot of the partying that accompanied most football weekends. But the practice worked, and our broadcasts were highly successful from that second game on.

This experience early in my broadcast career taught me an invaluable lesson, one that, incidentally, was a Boy Scout motto: Be prepared. For every story I expect to cover, I thoroughly research all the available material regarding the event, the background, and the major persons involved. And I don't design plans or labor-saving machinery that might permit me to skip this essential step in doing my job to the absolute limit of my ability. My motto is: There are no shortcuts to perfection.

William Harrison Jr.

FORMER CHAIRMAN AND CHIEF EXECUTIVE OFFICER, JPMORGAN CHASE

Known as the "great acquirer," William Harrison Jr. was responsible for the merging of a number of banks from Chemical Bank into Chase and then JPMorgan into Chase. He merged everything together and then retired in glory. Here we get a peek inside Harrison's JPMorgan, its in-house slogan, and the keys to success for all its employees.

William Harrison Jr., became chairman of JPMorgan Chase in 2005, prior to which he had been chairman and CEO since 2001. Harrison is also a director of Cousins Properties, Inc. and Merck & Co., Inc. He is a member of the Board of Overseers and Managers of Memorial Sloan-Kettering Cancer Center and of the Board of Directors of North Carolina Outward Bound and the Committee to Encourage Corporate Philanthropy.

BE A LEADER

Work hard. Take risks. Have a view. We came up with a
slogan for JPMorgan about three years ago: Be a leader.
We want everybody to be a leader. Some pundits say
that not everyone can be a leader, but in my view, everyone can be. To be a leader, you have to have a view,
be willing to constructively express it, and use it to make
something better. Under that definition, everybody can
be a leader. The lowest person in a company's hierarchy
ought to be doing that, and I'd argue that even the highest leader in the country has to do those things well; he
has to have a view, constructively express it, and get
people to follow him to make things better.

So my advice to young people is to have a view, go
make something better, get skin in the game, care about
it, and take some risks along the way. Taking risks is
very important. You shouldn't take crazy risks, but you
should take risks all the time to improve and to prove
yourself.

PRESIDENTIAL ADVICE

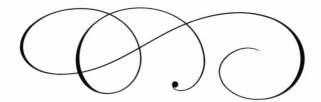

Gerald R. Ford

One of the most loyal and kind presidents to serve, Gerald R. Ford did what he felt was right to heal the country after the Nixon resignation. I visited with him a year before he died at his home in Palm Springs, where he reminisced about his old football days and his sadness that his knees had given out; it was difficult for him to walk in his old age. He still had that wonderful sense of humor and kindly grace that will probably make him one of the most respected presidents who served at a time when the nation needed to be set right. He displays that kindly grace in his letter, advocating respect for those whose ideas differ from our own.

Gerald R. Ford took the oath of office on August 9, 1974, in the aftermath of the Watergate scandal. He acted to curb the trend toward government intervention and spending as a means of solving the problems of American society and the economy.

OPPONENTS, NOT ENEMIES

I've always been an optimist, and still am. Yes, I suffered disappointments and defeats, but I tried to forget them and keep a positive attitude. When I was in sports and lost a game by error, or in the political arena, and lost by a narrow margin, no groaning would help. So I don't dwell on the past. I learned to move on and look ahead.

I can't stress enough how important this period of time is in your life. By forming good morals and learning the meaning of right and wrong now, you are setting a pattern that will follow you throughout life.

I encourage you to set goals and strive for excellence in all you do. The experience, knowledge, and discipline you acquire during your youth will be of immeasurable benefit in your adult life and how you affect your nation and its people.

I have had the privilege of working closely with Mrs. Ford, raising funds for the Betty Ford Center for Alcohol and Drug Abuse. I have seen firsthand how alcohol and drugs can affect one's life. It is so easy to slip into dependence. Therefore, I ask you not to give into peer pressure. It's okay to say no! Celebrate your life by being true to yourself.

Life is a gamble in anything you do, but challenges shouldn't dissuade you. I happen to believe if you prepare yourself and work hard toward a goal, you can achieve a certain degree of excellence and success.

Among the principles that a leader can never compromise is respect for others whose principles differ from their own. During my time in Congress and the White House, I often disagreed with people. I questioned their ideas—not their motives, and never their patriotism. I had opponents, but not enemies.

Good leaders are pragmatists. They want to make things work. They want to do the decent thing for others. When it comes to choosing leaders, we should value authenticity as much as ideology. Instead of following some demagogic person that distorts the truth, you should be informed on all sides of an issue and then be energized to be involved and to know all of the facts and ramifications. I am still convinced that truth is the glue that holds not only our government together, but also civilization.

Jimmy Carter

Jimmy Carter was a president whose deep faith guided his ways. Whether he felt things were right or wrong politically, his religious principles lead him in his decisions. In his letter he advocates expanding your world from your principle commitment to exploring new ideas, experiences, places, and people.

Upon graduation in 1946 from the Naval Academy, Jimmy Carter served for seven years as a naval officer. In 1962 he entered state politics, and eight years later he was elected governor of Georgia, emphasizing ecology, efficiency in government, and the removal of racial barriers during his administration.

Carter announced his candidacy for president in December 1974 and began a two-year campaign that ended with his defeat of Gerald R. Ford.

EXPAND YOUR HEARTS AND MINDS

I would say the main thing to remember is that no matter what you have as your primary commitment in life, try the ancillary things, the extra things that don't interfere with your major commitment, but that enhance and expand it. These have a tendency to also expand your hearts and your minds to encompass other people, which adds a new dimension to life. So I would say try new things. Don't restrict your lives. Don't live encapsulated in a cocoon just with people like you, who speak the same language, or look the same, or sing the same song, or worship the same way, but constantly explore new ideas and new experiences.

George H. W. Bush

FORTY-FIRST PRESIDENT
OF THE UNITED STATES

George H. W. Bush was one of the most principled, kind,
and dedicated presidents to serve. A man who cares
deeply about the United States and his loving family,
he has always shown respect for his son, the forty-third
president, even in the face of criticism. Your relationships
with those around you, he explains, are vitally important
to your success and happiness.

George H. W. Bush served two terms as a representative
to Congress from Texas and was appointed to a series of
high-level positions: ambassador to the United Nations,
chairman of the Republican National Committee, chief
of the U. S. Liaison Office in the People's Republic of
China, director of the Central Intelligence Agency. He
served two terms as vice president before winning the
1988 general election for president.

THE FORTY-FIRST PRESIDENT'S TOP TEN LIST

I cannot single out the one greatest challenge in my life. I have had a lot of challenges, and my advice to young people might be as follows:

1. Don't get down when your life takes a bad turn. Out of adversity comes challenge and often success.

2. Don't blame others for your setbacks.

3. When things go well, always give credit to others.

4. Don't talk all the time. Listen to your friends and mentors and learn from them.

5. Don't brag about yourself. Let others point out your virtues, your strong points.

6. Give someone else a hand. When a friend is hurt-ing, show that friend you care.

7. Nobody likes an overbearing big shot.

8. As you succeed, be kind to people. Thank those who help you along the way.

9. Don't be afraid to shed a tear when your heart is broken because a friend is hurting.

10. Say your prayers!!

George W. Bush

A president who believed in doing what he felt was right
for the country regardless of unpopular polls, George
W. Bush's approach to the security of the nation kept the
United States safe from another terrorist attack after 9/11.
His legacy to be determined by history, he firmly
believed his decisions were the right ones at the time
he made them. In his letter he suggests holding onto
a series of principles by which you can make decisions
and sticking by your decisions while trying to unite
people around those principles.

Prior to his presidency, George W. Bush served for six
years as the forty-sixth governor of Texas, where he
earned a reputation for bipartisanship and as a compassionate conservative who shaped public policy based on
the principles of limited government, personal responsibility, strong families, and local control.

SAY WHAT YOU BELIEVE AND STAND BY IT

September 11ᵀᴴ tested my ability to make decisions during a hectic period. History will judge whether or not I made the right decisions during a hectic period, but one thing September 11th did was to sharpen the skills necessary to be a good leader. Sometimes the toughest decisions have to be made when there's a lot of chaos, or seeming chaos, around.

I think a leader must have good instincts. One instinct that is important is the ability to judge the character of somebody else and determine the nature of that person.

One of the things we must do in America is to work for a culture that insists that people be responsible for the decisions they make in life. People should also understand that, in this country, a responsible society encourages people to love their neighbors.

Now, that's the way I was raised by my folks. We were taught that putting time in was noble and important. But my grandfather and grandmother also did a lot of charitable and volunteer work. I'm talking about something greater than public service; I'm talking about helping others in need. I believe that it's an important part of our society for people to contribute time and/or money to help those in need.

Here in Washington, it's important to know what you believe, base decisions upon principles, and not be afraid of what others think. I understand the office is bigger than the person. I'm a part of history, and it's a grand history, I might add.

Second, I believe deeply in freedom. I believe that freedom is not America's gift to the world; freedom is God's gift to every individual. I believe that a free society will be a peaceful society. I believe the human desire of every person on this globe is to be free. Those are, in my judgment, inherent American principles. And I make decisions based upon those principles and beliefs.

I trust people. I want people to be owners. I believe in an ownership society. That means that we have to close the minority gap in homes and encourage small-business creation.

I believe in local control where possible. The government that's closest to the people is that which can be reformed the most easily, if it needs to be reformed.

I understand whose money we spend in Washington. It's not the government's money; it's the people's money.

The role of government is not to create wealth but an environment in which the entrepreneur can flourish. Families are the backbone of a stable society, and public policy must reflect that.

In other words, there's a series of principles by which I make decisions—principles that came as a result of being raised where I was raised and by whom I was raised. It may seem like courage. To me it's natural to stick by the principles that are inherent in my being.

You have to say what you believe and stand by it. And it's tough in Washington, D.C., sometimes, because some people in this town are so political that they have a zero-sum attitude: Either I win and he loses, or he wins and I lose. That's not the way I think. I have Abraham Lincoln on the wall here in the Oval Office. He's on the wall because I think he was the country's greatest President, because he understood that a President must unite the country to achieve big objectives. And I worked hard to unite the country. We have to have a united country to achieve peace around the world and a united country to be a compassionate America. Therefore, you have to rise above the critics and the background noise here in Washington, speak directly to the people, and explain to them why we make the decisions we make. You have to bring them along in a constructive, nonpartisan way to achieve big things for this great country.

Lincoln had the hardest task of all, being President when the country was fighting internally. Yet, his whole thought process was aimed at the important principle of a United States of America, and he achieved that. I love to show people the portrait here in the Oval Office, and remind them that I am the President of the United States of America thanks to Abraham Lincoln.

LETTERS AND NUMBERS

Sumner Redstone

Sumner Redstone got his start as an owner of a group of small Massachusetts movie houses, eventually becoming executive chairman of Viacom, the parent company of Paramount Pictures and CBS. In his inspirational letter Redstone points out that opportunity does not knock, but with his "Three Cs," you can go out and grab it.

Sumner Redstone has been chairman of the board of National Amusements, Inc., since 1987, its CEO since 1967, and served as its president from 1968 through 1999. Redstone served as chairman of the board of the National Association of Theatre Owners and is currently a member of its executive committee. He has been a frequent lecturer at universities, including Harvard Law School, Boston University Law School, and Brandeis University. He graduated from Harvard University in 1944 and received an LLB from Harvard University School of Law in 1947.

THE THREE CS

I'm always looking for opportunities, both domestically and foreign. Opportunity does not knock. You have to find it. Nothing is impossible. Nothing. And then it's a matter of competence, commitment, and character. You have to have tremendous commitment to succeed. And you have to be highly competent to succeed. But without character you go nowhere.

I call them the three Cs: competence, commitment, and character. But without character, I'm not interested in competence and commitment.

I was born in a tenement. It made me want to succeed. Even when I was very young, going to Boston Latin School, I've always had a drive to try to be the best. It doesn't mean that I always have been. Whether it was a course at Boston Latin School, which was then the best school in the country, or whether it was practicing law, I've always had the same drive. You want to know where I get it? I don't know. Is it genealogical? Is it from our parents? I'm not sure. But I know that I started with a few drive-in theaters. And today I control the two best media companies in the world. So that is an achievement.

John Teets

A corporate executive who believes strongly in family and religion as moral compasses, John Teets built the Greyhound Corporation from a bus line into the Dial Corporation, a conglomerate that manufactures soap and food products. Through his appearances in company advertisements, he became famous for the greatest head of white hair in business. Three words, *positive mental attitude*, abbreviated to PMA, encapsulate his advice to us.

John Teets became chairman of the Greyhound Corporation in 1981 and restructured the company from a conglomerate into a profitable and streamlined company. In 1986 he was named "CEO of the Year" by *Leaders* magazine and received the National Human Relations Award from the American Jewish Committee. In 1990 he was given the *Forbes* magazine award for Top Business Speaker of the Year and Order of the Crown by the Kingdom of Belgium.

PMA

My first job at 10 years old was bailing out boats and selling worms. I vowed I would never be poor.

I am grateful for the success I have achieved and give credit to some of these philosophies I have held:

- Keep a positive mental attitude, or PMA.

- Think today is the first day of the rest of your life . . . Make the most of it.

- Be enthusiastic . . . it is an inside-out glow of mental energy.

- There is power in prayer.

- Common sense is not so common.

- Simple things confuse the wise.

- You can't learn anything if you are talking.

- Success comes in the "cans," not "cannots."

- Change your mind as often as new facts become available.

- Plan, act, and review.

- Lead, follow, or get out of the way.

- Always stay a green apple, because once you get ripe, someone will pick you. In other words, stay on the learning curve and exercise the mind.

Hopefully there will be a few nuggets of *inspiration* that you can adapt that will lead to your success.

Muriel "Mickie" Siebert

FOUNDER, CHAIRWOMAN, AND CHIEF EXECUTIVE OFFICER, MURIEL SIEBERT & CO., INC.

Muriel "Mickie" Siebert is known as the first woman of finance. Her road hasn't been easy. She was turned down by nine of the first ten men she asked to sponsor her application to become the first woman member of the Stock Exchange. But she prevailed and also became superintendent of New York State's banking department. She is a respected, scrappy, talented, strong-willed, and extremely knowledgeable person. Here she provides us with ten points on leadership and success to ponder.

After rising to partnership in a leading Wall Street brokerage firm, Muriel "Mickie" Siebert became the first woman member of the New York Stock Exchange in 1967, the year she founded her eponymous company. In 1977 she took five years off from her firm to serve as superintendent of New York State's Banking Department, with responsibility for the soundness of all New York banks.

THE FIRST WOMAN OF FINANCE'S TOP TEN

1. You create opportunities by performing, not complaining.

2. You see an opportunity and step up to the plate.

3. Take stands, take risks, take responsibility.

4. If you're not willing to accept the worst that can happen, don't do it.

5. Those who wait to see which way the wind is blowing will be unfurling their sails while the competition is crossing the finish line.

6. In any game where there are winners, there have to be losers, and it's no disgrace to lose. But you're not entitled to make the same mistake twice.

7. Any significant change in business is an opportunity for new business.

8. I believe in taking the Big Chance when it comes along. I follow my hunches, but before I act, I look at the numbers—inside out and upside-down.

9. I sleep well at night, knowing that I've been competitive but honest, tenacious but scrupulous, tough but fair.

10. Giving back is more than an obligation, it's a privilege.

Jean-Pierre Garnier

FORMER CHIEF EXECUTIVE OFFICER, GLAXOSMITHKLINE

Jean-Pierre Garnier helped merge pharmaceutical giants SmithKline Beecham and Glaxo Wellcome and is considered one of the most knowledgeable leaders in his field. Unlike many chief executive officers, he is not standoffish and his door is open to ideas from those inside and outside the company. Here he offers eight keys to the good life, and the blind pursuit of wealth is not one of them.

―――――――――

Jean-Pierre Garnier became CEO of GlaxoSmithKline in January 2001. Garnier serves on the boards of directors of the United Technologies Corporation, Committee to Encourage Corporate Philanthropy and the Eisenhower Exchange Fellowships, Inc. In 1997 he received France's Chevalier de la Légion d'Honneur and was promoted to Officier de la Légion d'Honneur in 2007. In April 1997 Garnier received the Oliver R. Grace Award for Distinguished Service in Advancing Cancer Research from the Cancer Research Institute. Garnier retired from Glaxo SmithKline in 2008.

EIGHT KEYS TO THE GOOD LIFE

1. Life is an adventure—live it accordingly!

2. Have a vision of what you'd like to be/to do. Be bold and don't let anyone talk you out of it. And then—just do it.

3. Family and friends are important; nothing else is truly long lasting. "Networking" and "social climbing" are for the weak. Be modest but self-assured.

4. To succeed, play on your strengths; they will compensate for what you don't have. It helps to be smart, but it helps more to be resilient and hard-working.

5. It's the journey that matters most; the destination is a big unknown. Be kind and generous and you will be paid back—most of the time.

6. Take time to "smell the roses" (take vacations!), exercise, and use your sense of humor and you will never burn out. A board meeting is less important than going to your child's school play!

7. Success in your profession is easy—success in your personal life requires 100 percent concentration.

8. John Lennon was right: Love is the answer.

Oswald J. Grübel

**FORMER CHIEF EXECUTIVE OFFICER,
CREDIT SUISSE GROUP**

An executive who never attended a university but instead earned his education through hard work within the banking and financial communities, Oswald J. Grübel guided the Credit Suisse Group with a down-to-earth style. Known for personally calling people instead of relying on his vice presidents, Grübel wanted to get things done, and fast. Although he writes in his letter about banking and finance, his wise words about achieving a feel for the future apply to any field.

———————

Oswald J. Grübel was the CEO of Credit Suisse Group and Credit Suisse until May 2007. He was CEO of Credit Suisse Financial Services from July 2002 to July 2004 and was also co–CEO of Credit Suisse Group from January 2003 until July 2004. Grübel was a member of the Credit Suisse Group Executive Board between 1997 and 2002.

75 PERCENT ABOUT THE FUTURE

I think the banking and finance businesses in general will be successful industries. But the requirements for young people to get into business today are much higher than they were ten years ago. You have to have a feel for the markets. Never mind understanding the business; anybody can learn that. What you cannot necessarily learn is that feeling for markets—knowing when things are changing and when public opinion is starting to change. I would say our business is at least 75 percent about the future. It's certainly not about the past, and it's not even very much about today. We continuously have to make decisions about the future.

James D. Robinson, III

GENERAL PARTNER, RRE VENTURES

As former chairman and chief executive officer of American Express, James D. Robinson III expanded the company's fame and fortune until it became a household name. He is now wealthy enough to run his own investment company, which has an excellent track record. He likes Italian food but somehow manages to stay skinny. In his letter to us he counts down his ten guidelines to good leadership.

———

Prior to cofounding RRE Ventures, James D. Robinson III worked for the American Express Company for twenty-three years, serving as chairman and CEO. He is a director of Bristol-Myers Squibb, where he also serves as chairman, the Coca-Cola Company, First Data Corporation, and Novell, Inc., and is a member of the Business Council, the Council on Foreign Relations, and the U.S.–Japan Business Council's executive committee.

LEADERSHIP, ONE THROUGH TEN

1. Surround yourself with people who are smarter than you. The smarter the people, the more you can accomplish.

2. Remember: Change is inevitable. Embrace it! Move with it! Drive it!

3. Listen. Be open to new ideas and alternative perspectives. You may find there is a better way of addressing an issue or building a business

4. Be passionate about whatever you do. Care intently about your work and feel personally accountable.

5. Get involved in your community. There are three important aspects of life: family, work, and the well-being of the community in which you live and work. It's called "enlightened self-interest." You will make yourself a more well-rounded executive.

6. Integrity matters around the clock. The same goes for humility. Check arrogance in any job at the door! Beware the illusions of success.

7. True leadership must have follower-ship. Management styles can vary, but even an autocrat needs people who believe and simply don't follow from fear.

8. Diversity is critical—by race, religion, age, and background. A well-integrated team made up of all those talents can be the best of the best.

9. The ability to communicate is critical, too—clearly, frankly, and often.

10. You can always learn from older, wiser heads who have years of experience. Too often people think someone who is older must be over the hill and not worth asking advice. Age brings wisdom—not always, but often.

Elias A. Zerhouni, M.D.

DIRECTOR,
NATIONAL INSTITUTES OF HEALTH

Overseeing an organization that tells the American
public about the dangers of disease and the necessity
of health can't be easy. But Elias A. Zerhouni. M.D. is a
"Dr. Diplomat" who does it very well. Here he gives
us his rules, based on a 50/50 principle. But watch out!
There are exceptions to every rule.

Elias A. Zerhouni, M.D., leads the National Institutes
of Health, the nation's medical research agency. In his
role as director, he oversees the NIH's 27 institutes and
centers, which have more than 18,000 employees and a
budget of $29.5 billion. The NIH investigates the causes,
treatments, and preventive strategies for both common
and rare diseases.

THE 50/50 RULES

I would like to share some of my personal rules of the road, which I crafted over the twenty-eight years since I graduated college. I call these rules my 50/50 rules.

My first rule is that 50 percent of what you learn is probably right and 50 percent is probably wrong. Your challenge is to figure out which is which.

Every day, whenever you hear about something new, ask yourself, "Which part makes sense and which requires caution and more work?" And always wonder how a stated fact could have been established.

It is not only fun to see the world this way; it is also a source of creativity, of seeking a different viewpoint. I deeply enjoy the feeling of discovering a new principle or relationship I had no idea about the previous day.

My second 50/50 rule is that more than half the time the answer to a problem is in an area of expertise other than your own. The history of science is full of such examples. Thus you should divide your learning 50/50 between your core discipline and concepts distant from it.

For example, I always made sure that 50 percent of what I read was in my field of radiology and 50 percent was in fields other than radiology.

My third 50/50 rule is that, at least in my experience, people become twice as smart when they are in the company of others—especially when those other people are smarter. You can rest assured that at least half of your intelligent contributions in life will be stimulated by others through cross-fertilization. You should seek and cultivate those interactions.

An illustration of this 50/50 rule is the remarkable number of scientific duos who have received Nobel prizes, such as James Watson and Francis Crick. Look at the legendary productivity of groups of scientists who came from famed laboratories such as the Cavendish. Discovery and creativity are eminently social processes.

My fourth 50/50 principle is to make sure you cultivate at least half of your colleagues and friends from beyond your own milieu. One of my closest friends who inspires me is an accountant!

Of course there are exceptions to my 50/50 rules.

First, never split your personal integrity. It should always be 100 percent. Your reputation is your only capital; do not risk it.

Second, in affairs of love I do not recommend the 50/50 approach. That would be deadly!

Finally, do not have half dreams! Just as surely as a small box cannot contain a larger one, so a full life cannot be contained in small dream box! In the end it is not failing that is painful, it is not having tried!

So make sure you have a big, bold, grand vision for yourself—and go for it!

Cathie Black

Cathie Black is one of the most powerful women in America. Tough and smart, she runs a $1.5 billion company profitably. How does she do it? Part of the answer can be found in her letter, in which she advises us to create our own definition of success and strive for a full array of life experiences around that definition.

Called the "First Lady of American Magazines" and "one of the leading figures in American publishing over the past two decades" by the *Financial Times*, Cathie Black heads Hearst Magazines, a division of Hearst Corporation and one of the world's largest publishers of monthly magazines. She manages some of the industry's best-known titles: *Cosmopolitan; Esquire; Good Housekeeping; Harper's BAZAAR; Marie Claire; O, The Oprah Magazine; Popular Mechanics; Redbook;* and *Town & Country*—19 magazines in all. Black has appeared on *Fortune* magazine's "50 Most Powerful Women in American Business" list each year since it debuted in 1998. She has also been included on *Forbes* magazine's list of the "100 Most Powerful Women."

LIVE A 360-DEGREE LIFE

The only definition of success that counts is your very own. There is no one way to succeed—no job or title or salary or recognition that says, "You've made it." Success is whatever makes you feel you're living with purpose.

When you define success for yourself, you remove pressure, feelings of inadequacy, and, worst of all, any attempt at trying to live up to someone else's expectations for you. To be truly independent is to be free of others' ideas of who you should be.

Live a 360-degree life—a full circle of experiences and people. Happiness is more important to success than success is to happiness. When you do what you love, in work and outside of work, and fill your world with family, friends, and community, you bring passion and joy to all you do and all you touch.

But it's not all about you. Every 360-degree life needs compassion, empathy, and service to make it meaningful. Use yours to make a difference. Make your happiness helpful. And on days when you're not feeling so happy, look ahead and move forward!

Howard J. Rubenstein

PRESIDENT,

RUBENSTEIN ASSOCIATES, INC.

Public relations expert Howard J. Rubenstein represents
some of the top individuals and organizations in the
United States, including the New York Yankees and
half the real estate moguls in New York and other large
cities. What he knows but never talks about could be
made into a movie. In his letter Rubenstein talks about
six tips that can provide a framework for success.

———————

Howard J. Rubenstein founded the firm that bears his
name in 1954. Since then he has served as a valued coun-
selor to some of the world's most influential corporations,
organizations, and opinion leaders. He has served as a
member of numerous civic and philanthropic organizations. He is vice-chairman of the Museum of Jewish
Heritage—A Living Memorial to the Holocaust and has
served as a consultant to the U.S. Foreign Claims Settle-
ment Commission and assistant counsel to the House Ju-
diciary Committee.

A FRAMEWORK

Over the last fifty years, I've had the privilege of working with clients who are leaders and pioneers. Based on that experience I would offer young people the following tips:

- Do the right thing. There are values that everyone knows but many disregard when it comes to business. Behave ethically. Work hard. Respect others. If you embrace this approach, it will make your reputation.

- Be conscientious. A true leader pays attention to details. It's often little things that derail a project. So, sweat the small stuff. At the same time, don't just act as an order taker. Bring your insight and ideas to the party.

- Don't be isolated in your thinking. Successful people are curious, willing to explore, and dedicated to their interests. Develop that characteristic by reading voraciously, staying on top of the news, and completing your education.

- Find a field that matches your personality and talent. Successful people love what they do. What you choose doesn't have to be glamorous or flashy. Find out what you want in life, work hard, and pursue your goals relentlessly.

- Be positive. We live in a cynical age with no shortage of naysayers. But there is more opportunity on the positive side: accomplishing and achieving things. Pursue your goals without tearing others down by gossiping or criticizing.

- Revere our nation's freedoms. I have seen so many success stories over the course of my career that could have happened only in America. The rights you have as an individual give you the freedom to pursue your dreams.

Take these tips as a framework to hang your ambitions and ideas on. And good luck. The world needs you.

Joseph H. Flom

SENIOR PARTNER, SKADDEN, ARPS, SLATE, MEAGHER & FLOM

Joseph H. Flom is certainly the most respected and sometimes feared lawyer in the United States. Companies would pay him a retainer of a million dollars a year just to keep him from being retained by others. He is one of the greatest litigating attorneys in the law profession, and he is highly respected, highly regarded, honest, and one of the most significant leaders of any law firm. As he explains in his letter, there is no single rule to achieving success, but acceptance of criticism, job satisfaction, innovative thinking, and not-for-profit work will aid your progress.

––––––––

Joseph H. Flom started his legal career as Skadden, Arps's first associate in 1948 and has led the firm as it has grown into one of the largest full-service law firms in the world. He is widely recognized as one of the leading attorneys practicing in the merger and acquisition arena, pioneering many of the strategies used today by bidders, targets, and investment bankers.

NO MAGIC FORMULA

The opportunities available for young people today are greater than they've been in the past because society is more open in terms of not having a ceiling on what you can accomplish. I am a good example of that. I grew up with extreme poverty, and with a little application and a little luck, here I am.

There are different kinds of opportunities: There are opportunities in professions. There are opportunities in corporations. You can't climb a ladder from the top, so you have to start at the bottom. The question is whether you have enough ambition and can put enough effort into trying to accomplish what your potential commits you to accomplish. Going to school advances you in a society that is more and more demanding of intellectual capacity and the pressure to use your intellectual capacity. But the opportunities are there in any field you choose, provided that you apply yourself and recognize that the efforts you put in today will pay off tomorrow.

I don't have any magic formula as to how to get ahead. However, I would say that you should recognize that criticism is not always a put down. If you take it to heart, maybe it will guide the way you ought to be going. And make sure that, early on, you get a job in an area that is satisfying to you so that you get pleasure out of doing whatever you are doing with an eye on advancing in that profession. It's a lot easier to advance if you're doing something you like. Also, you should try to go outside the box and, whatever you're doing, try to learn enough about the area so that you're one step ahead of the person next to you. This is something I practiced a great deal—to try to really understand what I was doing and to understand the collateral implications, because those are ways you can distinguish yourself from somebody who's just in the pack. Finally, I would not ignore the benefit of working with not-for-profit organizations which can use your services. Those are good for not only self-gratification, but also to give you access to other people in the community you can use for networking in terms of moving up.

PASSION AND JOB SATISFACTION

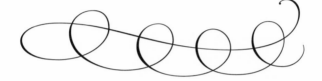

John F. Welch Jr.

FORMER CHIEF EXECUTIVE OFFICER, GENERAL ELECTRIC

John F. Welch Jr. is already a legend. He's straightforward, generous, and a brilliant character, and he would be the first one to admit that it's great to be a character. He loves what he's doing—writing, speaking, and having a great time *living*—even after his retirement from General Electric. Welch offers a series of wise statements about becoming a leader in a field that gives you satisfaction.

John F. Welch Jr. joined General Electric in 1960 and was elected vice president in 1972 and vice chairman in 1979. In 1981 he became the eighth chairman and chief executive officer in the company's 121-year history. He retired in the fall 2001. Welch is a former chairman and a member of both the Business Council and the National Academy of Engineering and is a member of the Business Roundtable.

SOMETHING THAT REALLY TURNS YOUR CRANK

Always look for opportunities that will give you a chance to learn. Don't be the last person to sign up. Always look for something that really turns your crank; look for work that you like and work that you want to do. Don't think of your career as a weigh station. Always over-deliver. Never do just what the boss asks; always do more. Have a positive attitude. Don't walk around with a sour face. No one wants that. Have a positive, can-do attitude. And have plenty of ambition, but don't wear it on your forehead when you're with your peers, subordinates, or superiors.

Maurice R. "Hank" Greenberg

CHAIRMAN AND CHIEF EXECUTIVE OFFICER, C.V. STARR & CO.

Maurice R. "Hank" Greenberg is a man with principal, someone who built a company from almost nothing to one of the largest in the world. He is a genius in business and even into his eighties is as sharp as a tack. He knows finance and business and is respected as a builder and creator on par with any of his contemporaries. While emphasizing the need to have passion in your endeavors, Greenberg explains how his success has been fostered by certain lessons and values he learned from his life experiences—growing up on a farm, serving in the military, and working in the insurance industry.

Maurice R. "Hank" Greenberg is the chairman and CEO of C.V. Starr & Co., Inc., and is the retired chairman and CEO of American International Group, Inc. (AIG). He is former chairman, and currently serves as a trustee, of the Asia Society. He is also chairman of the Starr Foundation, which provides major financial support to academic, medical, cultural, and public policy institutions.

PASSION

Whatever you choose to do, have passion for it. Don't try and hit a home run right out of the box. Stick with what you're good at, and if you're not good at it, don't do it. If you don't have passion for it, don't do it.

There are three parts in my life that have really influenced my own career. One was growing up on a farm and having the discipline that life on a farm gives you. Second, my experience in the military and being in two wars taught me a lot about people—who you can depend upon and who you can't. The discipline of the military also taught me about leadership; I started as a private and finished as a captain. And third, in the insurance industry, my background from both of those experiences led me to be consistent with what I try to do. I stick with things. My background provided me with leadership skills and a passion for what I do. If you're good at being a leader, it will show.

If you can't live through adversity, you'll never be good at what you do. You have to live through the unfair things, and you have to develop the hide to not let it bother you and keep your eyes focused on what you have to do.

Joseph R. Gromek

President and Chief Executive Officer, Warnaco Group

What does the head of a global apparel leader do for fun? He skis, which helps the blood pour back into his brain. And with a brain like Joseph R. Gromek's it helps him make money for Warnaco. Now Gromek has started a Warnaco Foundation to help in the education field. He's giving back, but in the meantime, he gets to wear all his own company's products from Calvin Klein, to Chaps, to even Speedo. Gromek says you should love what you do, and that will lead to diligence. Those things, combined with common sense and people skills, will lead to success.

Joseph R. Gromek has served as president and CEO of Warnaco since April 2003. At that time he was also elected to the Board of Directors. From 1996 to 2002, he served as president and CEO of Brooks Brothers, Inc. He has held senior management positions with Saks Fifth Avenue, Limited Brands, Inc., and AnnTaylor Stores Corporation. Gromek is the chairman of the Board of Directors of Volunteers of America and a member of the Board of Governors of the Parsons School of Design.

THE FIRST PLACE TO START

Obviously it's important to like what you're doing, and even more important to love what you're doing. So that's the first place to start. If you love what you're doing, you're going to work diligently, and ultimately, I believe you will be successful. Common sense is also very important in our business. People skills are very important, and treating people the way you want to be treated is essential for success.

The world today operates as a meritocracy; there are no limits to what you can accomplish. Set your sights on something, have goals, have aspirations, and work diligently toward them, and ultimately they can be achieved.

A GLOBAL SUMMIT

The Dalai Lama

The Dalai Lama is a religious leader of noble and simple
principles without the pomp of other religious icons. He
cares deeply about Tibet and is fascinating to listen to.
During lunch one day he explained to me the steps of
enlightenment and how at the highest level he is able
to transfer thoughts and heal others. A modest, gentle,
kindly soul, he explains in his letter that while the purpose of life—happiness—may seem like a selfish one, the
best way to achieve it is through working for the benefit
of others, the most selfless act we can perform.

His Holiness the Fourteenth the Dalai Lama Tenzin
Gyatso, is the head of state and spiritual leader of the
Tibetan people. He has been living in Dharamsala,
northern India, the seat of the Tibetan political administration in exile. In 1989 His Holiness was awarded the
Nobel Peace Prize for his nonviolent struggle for the lib-
eration of Tibet.

LOVE AND COMPASSION

One great question underlies our experience, whether we think about it consciously or not: What is the purpose of life? I believe that the purpose of life is to be happy. From the moment of birth, every human being wants happiness and does not want to suffer. From the very core of our being we simply desire satisfaction. Therefore, it is important to discover what will bring about the greatest degree of happiness.

From my own limited experience, I have found that the greatest degree of inner tranquility comes from the development of love and compassion. The more we care for the happiness of others, the greater becomes our own sense of well-being. Cultivating a close, warm-hearted feeling for others automatically puts the mind at ease. This helps remove whatever fears or insecurities we may have and gives us the strength to cope with any obstacles we encounter. It is the ultimate source of success in life.

As long as we live in this world, we are bound to encounter problems. If at such times we lose hope and become discouraged, we diminish our ability to face difficulties. If, on the other hand, we remember that it is not just ourselves but everyone who faces hardships of one kind or another, this more realistic perspective will increase our determination and capacity to overcome our troubles. Indeed, with this attitude each new obstacle can be seen as yet another valuable opportunity to improve our mind! Thus, we can strive gradually to become more compassionate, that is we can develop both genuine sympathy for others' suffering and the will to help remove their pain. As a result, our own serenity and inner strength will increase.

I believe that to meet the challenge of our times, human beings will have to develop a greater sense of universal responsibility. It is only this feeling that can remove the self-centered motives that cause people to deceive and misuse one another. If we have sincere and open hearts, we will naturally feel self-worth and confidence and there will be no need to be fearful of others. The key to a happier world is the growth of compassion. We do not need to become religious, nor do we need to believe in an ideology. What is necessary is for each of us to develop our good human qualities. We must all learn to work not just for our own self, family, or nation, but for the benefit of all humankind.

Mikhail Gorbachev

The man who transformed the Soviet Union is revered more outside Russia than within the country. He did tear down the Berlin Wall, and in my conversations with him he continually praised Ronald Reagan and talked of his respect for the former president. He felt they became close friends and could trust each other. In his letter he calls us to join in a common effort with family, friends, and all citizens of planet Earth to handle the challenges we face as a human race.

Mikhail Gorbachev became general secretary of the Soviet Union in 1985. He initiated the process of change in the Soviet Union—what was later called *perestroika*, the fundamental transformation of the nation and society. Gorbachev played a prominent role in ending the Cold War, stopping the arms race, and eradicating the threat of a nuclear war. He was awarded the Nobel Peace Prize in October 1990. Since March 1993 he has been president of Green Cross International.

ALL PEOPLE ARE BRETHREN

My young friend,

You have your whole life ahead. This is the life that you will have to live, and this should be a dignified life. What is the way to do this? One can never teach others as to what is the right way to live. Each has to make his or her own choice. And everyone's destiny will have its ups and downs, its zigzags, drawbacks, and accomplishments.

But all of us are steered to the path of life by our mother and father and by the family. No matter what, the family is called upon to continue as your most reliable support. But mind you: It also depends on you whether or not your family remains your support.

Another support in life comes from your friends, the people who will be with you all your life long. True, they all differ a lot. But as long as you have them, you are never lonely. This means that there is someone at your side, someone who extends a helping hand, someone who gives support and consolation when you need it. Make sure that your friends are important to you. Make sure that people are important to you.

In their younger days all people are asking them-selves what profession they should choose and what their annunciation can be. What they should choose to get is success and well-being and to become a person that other people and society need. When a person has no vocation in life and is not wanted, it makes him suf-fer. The right choice that matches your inclinations, capabilities, and tastes is the cornerstone of your entire life.

But whatever the choice, all people have to withstand all kinds of tests in their lives. It stands to reason that in many respects these tests are individual, too. But at a time like ours, they are increasingly becoming common to all of us.

Indeed, we do speak different languages. We have different colors of skin. We belong to religions of differ-ent denominations or remain atheists. But in spite of all these things, we are facing the same challenges today. And these are challenges many of which we, people, have generated. These are the challenges of wars and violence that are taking a heavy toll of life. This is the challenge coming from the badly wounded nature that is urging us to care and help. This is the challenge com-ing from terrorism and crime. This is the challenge of dreaded diseases that, for the time being, are hard to cure. And, certainly, this is the challenge coming from poverty and illiteracy that lays the groundwork for the tragedies of millions of people who need support and compassion.

Everyone, including you, can and must contribute his or her share of effort, thought, and action in order to find answers to these dramatic challenges. But it is only through a common effort that we can solve the emergent challenging problems. All people are brethren—this is a maxim known from times immemorial. Unfortunately, the citizens of the planet Earth have not always behaved as brethren. Now it is high time that we recalled this great truth drawing us away from one another. We have to join our efforts together for the sake of the future.

The future is always something unknown. No doubt, it will yield us great many new, unusual, and so far unknown things. But the future begins now. We are witnessing it being brought into existence by our own efforts. And what will happen to us tomorrow depends on what all of us are doing now, in our own capacity.

And I am saying to you, to all young citizens of the Earth: Be brave, persistent, and efficient. Do not be afraid of life. Life is beautiful because it is life. But it can be better, and it will become better if all of us want it—if we do our best in order to preserve and increase the wealth that was bestowed on us by nature and by people's labor.

And it's my wish that in the end of the chosen path that each of you could say: "I've lived my life and it was not in vain. And I am happy!"

Vladimir Putin

FORMER PRESIDENT AND CURRENT PRIME MINISTER OF RUSSIA

Some say he was a strong dictator but, after all, as head of Russia his job was to advance Russia's interests above those of other nations. I found him to be completely charming with a great sense of humor and a devoted father to his two daughters. At the end of his call to the world's youth to actively engage in economic and cultural change, Putin leaves us with an age-old recipe for success.

Vladimir Putin rose through the ranks of the KGB and then the Russian government to become president of Russia in 2000. On March 14, 2004, he was elected to a second term. Since May 8, 2008, Putin has been a prime minister of Russia.

DILIGENCE IS THE MOTHER OF SUCCESS

This generation is not the first—or the last—to face problems and difficulties, including those of an international character. Everyone knows how much the peoples of the world suffered during the last century, which saw the massive tragedy of World War II. Today we are facing a new threat: the threat of terrorism. Unfortunately no country—not even the strongest power—is able to insulate itself from this threat. We should all concentrate on the fight against international terror, and the youth can't stand aloof, putting all their hopes in their governments. I am convinced that youth organizations should consider their potential input into the fight against extremism, violence, racism, and religious intolerance.

Today young people represent one of the most active and mobile groups in societies around the world. It is no coincidence that younger citizens are actively involved in international humanitarian, intellectual, and cultural projects. This is largely facilitated by modern information technology, the common values of freedom and democracy, and the open policies of states. Young people can now communicate easily, develop business relationships, and make new friends. Obviously all of this helps them find their place in life, receive a good education, and apply their abilities to pursue their ambitions. And, at the same time, they can make their own contributions to the development of our world: its economy and culture.

As for any specific advice, I know a very old, time-tested recipe for success. Our ancestors came up with it hundreds of years ago: Diligence is the mother of success. I am sure that remains relevant today.

Roh Tae Woo

FORMER PRESIDENT OF THE REPUBLIC OF KOREA

Roh Tae Woo was the first president of Korea to try to bring the North and South Korean governments together. It's because of him that these discussions have any chance of continuing. Bold measures are always risky, as Roh relates in his letter about his presidency. Yet the risks can be well worth the reward, sometimes historically worth the reward.

Roh Tae Woo was the thirteenth president of South Korea (1988–1993). He was handpicked by the ex-general Chun Doo Hwan to succeed him as president, triggering large pro-democracy rallies in Seoul and other cities in 1987. In response, Roh agreed to hold democratic presidential elections, and he became the first democratically elected president after the end of military rule. Roh Tae Woo will be remembered for the broad political reform that he helped start, steering the country toward greater democracy and pluralism.

AUDACIOUSLY REALIZE FORMULATED DECISIONS

The greatest challenge in my life was the presidential election in which I ran. At the time I was named a presidential candidate, Korea's president was to be selected through an indirect election, which by nature favors the ruling party. As a candidate from the ruling party, I was sure to eventually become president.

At that time, however, the Korean people had long been aspiring to cast their direct votes to elect their president. During the phenomenal economic development since the 1960s, some of the basic civil rights had to be neglected, and the Korean people were hoping for the realization of a more perfect democracy.

In the view of my supporters, the democratization measures were not easy to accept and implement. Enormous disadvantages and setbacks were foreseen. I was agonizing between the anticipated honor of presidency and the nation's aspirations for democratization. But I soon realized that the times demanded that I bolster democracy in Korea and eliminate the threat of a war from the Korean peninsula.

After days of deep contemplation, I concluded that a presidency that would be ignored by the people and by history would he meaningless, and I made up my mind to give up all favorable conditions guaranteed to me until then.

As a result, I decided to implement numerous reform measures such as direct universal suffrage through revising the constitution in order to enable all politically restricted activists to run for the presidency so long as they are Korean nationals and guaranteeing full freedom of the press. Those measures could be called "revolutionary" at the time.

It was none other than the "June 29 Declaration," which I put forward on that date in 1987. Consequently, the Korean people praised and supported me—one who dared to take on the unfavorable circumstances—and elected me as the thirteenth president of the Republic of Korea.

"The June 29 Declaration" is now on record as being an important catalyst for Korea's democracy having taken firm root. More specifically it is credited with laying the foundation for Korea to become a role-model democracy while simultaneously becoming one of the ten greatest trading nations in the world since it was rebuilt from the ashes of the Korean War.

After my inauguration as president, even more challenges were awaiting me. Vis-à-vis North Korea, I adopted a detour strategy, by which we would impel the North to enter into dialogues by first establishing friendly relations with China and the then–Soviet Union, longtime allies of the North.

The springboard for that strategy was the Seoul Olympic Games, among the greatest of its kind in history. The Olympics had been paralyzed amid conflicts between the free world and the communist bloc. I strived to heal the wounds inflicted upon the world by the rift between East and West and urged North Korea into the world community by making the Olympiad a true festival of mankind in the divided land of Korea.

During the process, North Korea's resistance was beyond description, and I was also burdened with the task of persuading the South Korean people, who abhorred the specter of communism. Fortunately the Seoul Olympics proved to be as resounding a success as had been intended, and we were able to normalize relations with East European countries such as Hungary, the then–Soviet Union, and China. Subsequently, we started dialogue with North Korea and signed the South-North Basic Agreement and the Joint Denuclearization Declaration with the North, thereby drastically reducing the risk of a war on the Korean peninsula. This policy I developed is called *Nordpolitik* in reference to the *Ostpolitik* of Willy Brandt, the West German premier.

Lastly, I would like to tell all young readers of this book that a supreme leader who truly loves his or her people should be able to sacrifice him- or herself, persuade the people, and audaciously realize formulated decisions, with the conviction that he or she would take historical responsibilities.

King Abdullah II

KING OF JORDAN

Like his father, King Abdullah II is known as the "quiet peacemaker." For years he has been a conciliator between Arab nations that don't always get along—even between the United States and Israel in their relations with the Arab world. The respect King Abdullah II garners from the international community allows him to be a carrier of top-level messages.
Confidence and a positive attitude, His Majesty explains in his letter, will put you in a position to succeed no matter what challenges lie ahead.

King Abdullah II bin al-Hussein is the forty-third generation direct descendant of the Prophet Muhammad (Peace Be Upon Him). He took on his constitutional powers as monarch of the Hashemite Kingdom of Jordan on February 7, 1999. Since then, he has played a strong and positive moderating role within the Arab region and the world and has worked toward a just and lasting solution to the Arab-Israeli conflict.

PROVIDE LEADERSHIP THROUGH COURAGE

A school teacher, a farmer, a soldier, an athlete, a mother, and an entrepreneur can provide leadership when they decide to confront the challenges of life with honesty, courage, determination, and a sense of optimism.

I have always found that one's confidence and positive attitude in dealing with issues, challenges, and difficulties usually secure over half of the victory in the battle to succeed. This is true, regardless of the scope or complexity of the issues.

So my advice to the young generation is for them to always provide leadership through courage, and to always focus on doing the correct thing in life. These are basic facts that we all, I suppose, learnt at kindergarten. But they remain valid for all of us as we struggle through life to make a difference for the poor, hungry, and oppressed and to provide meaning to life, one that is full of hope, promise, and success.

Mohamad Mahathir

FORMER PRIME MINISTER
OF MALAYSIA

During Mohamad Mahathir's time as prime minister, Malaysia had tremendous success. Because of his strong personality, he was an extremely effective government leader. As they used to say, "Don't mess with him." In his letter he discusses the challenges of changing the values of those around us.

Mahathir bin Mohamad became the fourth prime minister of Malaysia in 1981, and he served in this position until 2003. During the 1970s he held several ministerial posts, including minister of education and minister of trade and industry. In 1973 Mohamad was appointed as a senator, and in 1975 he was elected as one of the three vice presidents of his party. In 1976 he served as deputy prime minister and won the deputy president seat in 1978. In 1981 he was appointed president of his party.

IT'S WORTH TRYING

Young people must remain optimistic, and they must hold onto their ideals. We should motivate them to strive to change the world for the better. Of course later on in life they are going to find that their ideals are not so easily followed, but knowing that does not mean that they shouldn't try. After all, maybe they will succeed in making a difference.

When I was very young, I believed it would be very easy to change things. It turns out that I was a bit naïve. I thought I could change people's values for the better, but after many years of trying, I've had very little success in that area. Generally speaking, you cannot change people as quickly as you might like to, but nevertheless, I would say it's worth trying. For me, it has certainly been worth the effort, and I am content with the little success I have achieved in this area.

Nursultan Nazarbayev

PRESIDENT OF KAZAKHSTAN

Nursultan Nazarbayev is a man of strong principles
but with tremendous charm. Although he didn't speak
English when I met him in Kazakhstan, his sense of
humor made me feel right at home, even in translation.
He is dedicated to building up Kazakhstan and has great
support of the people. Nazarbayev gives us the question
we must answer in the affirmative every evening in our
efforts to find harmony and success.

Nursultan Nazarbayev, a doctor in economics, worked
his way up through the Soviet political system and from
1984 to 1989 was a chairman of the Ministers Council
of the Kazakh Soviet Socialist Republic. From 1989 to
1991 he served as first secretary of the Central Committee of the Communist Party of Kazakhstan. From February to April 1990, he concurrently served as chairman
of the Supreme Council of the Kazakh Soviet Socialist
Republic. Since April 1990 he has been president of the
Republic of Kazakhstan.

DID I LIVE THIS DAY RIGHT?

Every man's life is full of twists of fate and tests of one's strengths. It is not without reason that the main thing people ask for in their prayers is: "Save me from evil and bad luck."

Having given man intellect, the Creator put in front of him an eternal choice between good and evil, light and darkness, love and hate, knowledge and ignorance.

It seems like all kind of problems arise with the single purpose of having a man overcome obstacles and find optimal ways to achieve his goals. Therefore, adequate assessment of the situation and making a correct decision are always a source of progress.

True happiness comes when a man chooses the best of possible options at every moment of his life and, through that, achieves harmony with the world and himself.

Success will always be with young people if they choose humanism, knowledge, responsibility, fairness, and unselfishness as their allies. That is the crux of my credo.

This is the reason why every evening I try to answer an important question: "Did I live this day right?"

For me, as the president, the question also means, "Am I doing all I can to improve the life of my people?"

Lee Hsien Loong

PRIME MINISTER, SINGAPORE

Lee Hsien Loong's father, the first prime minister of
Singapore, made Singapore a great country and a
great business center. Now the son is carrying on the
tradition. Lee Hsien Loong survived cancer, is a health
enthusiast, and is sharp as a tack, perhaps as sharp as
his father. And here he speaks to the responsibility
of each succeeding generation to carry on the work
of those who came before them.

Lee Hsien Loong was sworn in as Singapore's third
prime minister in 2004, has served multiple terms as a
member of Parliament, and has held various other roles
in Singapore's government: Minister for Trade and Industry, Second Minister for Defence, Chair of the Economic Review Committee, Chairman of the Monetary
Authority of Singapore, and Deputy Prime Minister.
As prime minister, Lee has launched policies to build a
competitive economy and an inclusive society.

TO BUILD A COUNTRY FROM SCRATCH

Unlike the United States, a large country over two centuries old, Singapore is a very small and young country—one-fifth the size of Rhode Island. It had a traumatic birth in 1965 when it was expelled from Malaysia. Few international observers expected the tiny island city-state to survive, let alone succeed.

So my parents' generation had to build a country from scratch. They overcame long odds to develop Singapore into a middle-income nation, attaining in one generation a standard of living that took other countries decades to achieve.

My generation experienced this transformation in our lives as we grew up. We knew that our progress was an act of will and that we could not take further progress for granted. We strived to build upon what we had inherited, to make Singapore a vibrant business hub and a resilient, dynamic society.

Singapore's youth today grow up with the benefits and opportunities that their parents and grandparents had labored to provide them. But they have not had a free ride. They have witnessed the Asian Crisis, the global threat of extremist terrorism, and the outbreak of the deadly SARS virus. They are experiencing the formidable challenges of global competition, but also the excitement of Asia on the move. They are ambitious to remake their world, to prosper in a global economy, and to create a brighter future for themselves.

It is hard to tell what tomorrow's Singapore will be like. This is for all young Singaporeans to shape and build. It is easy to describe what we want—a cosmopolitan city, yet one firmly rooted in our Asian cultures; an open society welcoming diverse views, yet cohesive and with a sense of national purpose; a competitive economy that offers opportunities for the able and enterprising and delivers high and rising standards of living for all; and a political system that produces honest, capable leadership and enjoys popular support and the mandate to guide the country forward.

Our challenge is to realize these aspirations. Each generation has to solve its own problems and prepare the next generation to solve its problems. Each should leave its country, and the world, a better place than before. This is my goal, too.

GLOBALIZATION

G. Allen Andreas

FORMER CHAIRMAN AND
CHIEF EXECUTIVE OFFICER, ADM

G. Allen Andreas took a successful company, one of the world's largest agricultural processors, and expanded it worldwide—even into China. A forward-looking leader, he was influential in creating alternative fuels and energy and planning for the future health of the company in the face of environmental changes taking place in our world. Education, he explains, especially technological and linguistic education, is the key to success in today's global village.

G. Allen Andreas served as an attorney for the U.S. Treasury Department from 1969 until joining the legal staff of the Archer Daniels Midland Company in 1973. Appointed treasurer in 1986, Andreas relocated to Europe in 1989 as CFO of European Operations and returned to the United States in 1994 as vice president and counsel to the Executive Committee. He was appointed a member of the Office of the Chief Executive in 1996, president and chief executive officer in 1997, and chairman and chief executive in January 1999.

THE GREATEST EDUCATION POSSIBLE

In today's world, you need to get the greatest education possible, because technology is driving so much change in everyone's businesses. So you need to become as fully educated as possible, and obtain global experience. Language skills are very significant assets in today's world and they will allow you to be entrepreneurial in spirit and to be able to move to locations where your skills are needed most. Language skills will also allow you to move within the system in order to maximize your own talents. That's a key to success in any global business today.

Lee Kuan Yew

Lee Kuan Yew built a country from scratch following World War II. He's revered throughout the world by other heads of state. During my yearly visits he would predict what would happen the following year, and he was right about 90 percent of the time. A man with amazing mental capacity, he is spot-on in his letter as he explains that taking on the challenges of globalization is as vital to individuals and organizations as it is to entire countries.

Lee Kuan Yew led Singapore to independence and served as its first prime minister. He was reelected time and again from 1959 until he stepped down in 1990. Under his guidance Singapore became a financial and industrial powerhouse despite a lack of abundant natural resources. After stepping down in 1990, Lee was succeeded as prime minister by Goh Chok Tong. Lee remained in the cabinet as senior minister.

THE OPPORTUNITIES OF GLOBALIZATION

This is an unfair world. Some countries are rich, many are poor. Globalization may make it more unfair by widening the gap between them. But if you position your country to make the most of the opportunities of globalization, you will do better then those who do not.

Donald J. Trump

What needs to be said about the Donald?
Nobody can say it better than Donald J. Trump himself,
especially when it comes to globalization.

Donald J. Trump is the world's most famous business-
man, a best-selling author and media personality, and a
symbol of success for people around the world. He is also
the founder of Trump University, which teaches success
principles and financial independence.

THE WORLD IS A BIG PLACE

My best advice today for young people starting their careers is to be globally aware. This requires a daily discipline of keeping up with worldwide events, as well as national and local events. You must know what's going on in the world to be an effective member of the world. My father always said to me, "Know everything you can about what you're doing" and I have followed his advice.

Being a leader means being prepared. That also means being prepared to never give up. Being tenacious with your goals is absolutely necessary. Great success rarely comes easily. Even today I encounter problems every day, but I remain positive, disciplined, and focused. Approach every day that way and it's likely you will succeed. Adversity is very often an opportunity in disguise.

I am listed in the *Guinness Book of World Records* for having the biggest financial turnaround in history. I owed billions of dollars in the early 1990s and many people thought I was finished. Even the newspapers were announcing my demise. The difference is that I didn't believe I was finished for one second, no matter what people thought. I simply refused to give in to negative circumstances and I kept working. In short, I refused to give up. I am now far more successful than I ever was.

The world is a big place. Think accordingly, be prepared, and never give up. That's a great combination for success. Work hard and good luck!

WISDOM INHERITED

Anton Rupert

Anton Rupert lived in South Africa, where he loved wine making. His Stellenbosch Wineries have become a brand name for the finest in South African wines. He also put together a company that owns Cartier, Dunhill, Montblanc, Van Cleef & Arpels, Piaget, Vacheron Constantin, Jaeger-LeCoultre, and IWC. What a combination! In his letter Rupert gives us a wonderful blend of his favorite proverbs.

South African industrialist and philanthropist Anton Rupert passed away in 2006, but his legacy lives on. He built a small tobacco company into a huge multinational conglomerate that encompasses hundreds of businesses in several countries. In 1948 he renamed his company Rembrandt, which became the core of a financial empire. Rupert was a founding member of the World Wildlife Fund (WWF) and in 1997 became a founding patron of the Peace Parks Foundation, which was created to establish cross-border conservation parks in southern Africa.

PROVERBS

- He who does not believe in miracles is not a realist.

- It is better to light a small candle than to curse the darkness.

- Where there is a will there is a way; the will itself becomes the way.

- For every crisis, for every fear, for every problem, there is the reverse side of an opportunity.

- We can only make ourselves indispensable through service and achievement.

- Always put yourself in the other man's shoes; also consider his point of view.

- What you do to others will be done to you.

- Worrying is like a rocking chair, it keeps you busy but it brings you nowhere.

- No good deed ever goes unpunished.

- Let us use the past as a springboard to the future, not as a rocking chair.

Gerhard Schröder

FORMER CHANCELLOR, GERMANY

One of Germany's most charismatic chancellors, Gerhard Schröder has a terrible temper but a great sense of humor. In his letter he cites no less a luminary than Immanuel Kant to deliver his wisdom to the future leaders of the world.

Gerhard Schröder studied law at Göttingen University before entering politics. Long affiliated with the Social Democratic Party, he was elected chancellor in 1998, unseating the incumbent Helmut Kohl after sixteen years in office. After stepping down as chancellor in 2005, Schröder accepted a post as the head of the shareholder's committee in a Russian-led consortium, controlled by the gas company Gazprom, which is building a pipeline from Russia to Germany.

THE CATEGORICAL IMPERATIVE

Be self-confident. Never give up. Always have a plan. Remain firmly committed to your goals and values, even if you encounter some opposition. And don't let yourself be discouraged if a particular project doesn't work. And, if I may say this as a "child of European enlightenment": Stick to Kant's "Categorical Imperative": Act so that the maxim of your action may be capable of becoming a universal law for all rational beings.

Leo Hindery Jr.

MANAGING PARTNER,
INTERMEDIA PARTNERS

An expert in media of all kinds, Leo Hindery Jr.,
is considered in television and print to be one of the
most far-seeing investors. What he has touched in
the past has pretty much turned to gold. Riffing off
a quotation from Napoleon, here Hindery explains
what it takes to be a leader.

Leo Hindery Jr., is managing partner of InterMedia
Partners, a major private equity firm. Prior to starting
InterMedia Partners, Hindery was CEO of the YES
Network, the nation's premier regional sports network,
which he helped form in 2001 as the television home of
the New York Yankees and the New Jersey Nets. Previously he has been chairman and chief executive officer of
GlobalCenter Inc., president and chief executive officer
of AT&T Broadband, and president and chief executive
officer of Tele-Communications, Inc. (TCI). Hindery is
also the author of *The Biggest Game of All*.

METEORS WHO LIGHT OUR WORLD

Napoleon said that, "Great men are meteors, consuming themselves to light the world." The same can be said of great leaders.

And those rare individuals who rise to be genuine leaders of their generation, those meteors who light our world, have specific unassailable characteristics which distinguish and in turn define them.

A great leader needs to love and respect people, and he needs to be comfortable with himself and with the world. He also needs to be able to forgive himself and others. In other words, a leader needs to have "grace."

A great leader must have a deep reservoir of knowledge and broad perspectives. He must be bright and at once both outward and forward looking.

Along with grace and cleverness comes "vision," and a woman or man without a vision is not a leader. One must always know with great clarity where one wants to go and why.

A leader cannot lead without being able to articulate his vision. This means having the ability first to think straight and then to express thoughts and ideas clearly and directly. And a leader must give brain and heart equal access to his tongue.

A leader has to be completely comfortable in making decisions and needs to understand the imperative of making informed and timely ones. He can't be timid or shallow; many people are waiting and counting on leaders, and sometimes even a nation is. President Harry Truman said that the ultimate test of any decision is "not whether it's popular at the time, but whether it's right. If it's right, make it, and let the popular part take care of itself."

Thomas Edison said that genius—and he certainly was one—is 10 percent inspiration and 90 percent perspiration. But Edison was also a great leader, some even say the "CEO of the Century," and he knew and said that the same applies to leadership. You've got to be hard-working. There's simply no other way to get the job done and to inspire others to also give their utmost.

Finally, no entity that I ever want to be part of can tolerate a leader who isn't, deep in his core, honest and ethical—and being ethical is not some organizational or political expediency developed later in life. Ethics are formed over a lifetime starting at a very young age.

So, there you have it, the requirements for a great leader: grace, broad intelligence, vision, the ability to articulate ideas, reasoned and timely decision making, hard work, and ethics.

And because I am privileged to be a businessperson, I want to say that a particular imperative for genuine success in business leadership is acknowledging and embracing equal and concurrent responsibility to constituencies other than only shareholders or owners. A business leader has just as much obligation to employees, customers, and communities as he or she does to shareholders—and larger companies and their executives also have a strong common responsibility to the nation.

Wendelin Wiedeking, the great chief executive of Porsche, spoke compellingly to this point when he said that, as businesspeople "we should not always look at getting the maximum return, but we must look at people and make sure they are [also] taking part. We also have to pay a lot of attention to our customers, for when the customer is happy, then the worker is happy and so are the suppliers—and then there should be enough money left for the shareholders. I have never understood shareholder value [only], as it leaves so many things out. Shareholders give their money just once, whereas the employees work every day."

Leslie E. Bains

VICE CHAIRMAN, MODERN BANK
AND CHIEF EXECUTIVE OFFICER,
MODERN ASSET MANAGEMENT

Leslie E. Bains has had many careers in volunteering, business, and finance and just as many serving on the boards of nonprofit organizations. Her two children went to Duke University, and she's helping the school's medical center. She combines smart with serve—a good combination. A vision of something greater than yourself, Bains explains in her letter, attracts others to your missions. As a great philosopher put it, it's all about having a *why* that's more than just money or fame.

———————————

Prior to joining Modern Bank, Leslie E. Bains was president of AFS Intercultural Programs, one of the world's largest nonprofit, community-based volunteer organizations. She retired at the end of 2003 as senior executive vice president of HSBC North America, where she was the highest-ranking woman and member of the senior management committee. She also held executive posts with JP Morgan/Chase and Citibank.

A WHY TO LIVE

Over the years I have had the pleasure to work with many successful leaders in both the business and non-profit sectors. I have learned that successful leaders are those who have a vision of something greater than themselves.

If you chase after money or status, chances are you'll have a hard time catching up with them. But when you have a vision that goes beyond your own needs, people will naturally want to be part of it, and no idea, no matter how great, ever became a reality without the as-sistance of many hands—this is equally true in business as in public service or the arts.

A philosopher once said, "He who has a *why* to live can bear almost any *how*." I would add, "He who has a why to *lead* can bear almost any trial."

Jean Afterman

VICE PRESIDENT AND ASSISTANT GENERAL MANAGER, NEW YORK YANKEES

Ten years ago it would have been unheard of for a woman to be involved in running the New York Yankees. Jean Afterman has a great sense of humor, is tough but nice, and has great communication skills (she used to teach English before she became a lawyer). As an agent for players, she helped bring the first baseball player from Japan's major league to an American big league club. Now she's in charge of international brand expansion for the Yankees . . . and she gets great seats at the games. In her letter she addresses a golden nugget of advice she read in *The Diary of Anne Frank*.

Jean Afterman is only the third woman to hold her current position in Major League Baseball. Prior to joining the Yankees, she provided athletic representation and management with a specialization in arbitration proceedings. From 1994 to 1999, she was general counsel at KDN Sports, Inc., and handled business and legal affairs for international baseball clients.

THE FINAL FORMING OF YOUR CHARACTER

My mother's mother emigrated from Riga and came to the United States in about 1905. In her seventies, she already spoke four languages when she decided that she wanted to learn Spanish. And she did—she attended classes and practiced with Spanish speakers around her. The lesson for me was, and is, that education should never cease, no matter what age or where you are. And there are lessons to be had not only in formal education, but in everything you do.

When I was fourteen years old, I was attending a terrific school, with inspirational teachers—we read the curriculum that was generally being read at the time (and I believe is still somewhat the same). One of the books was *The Diary of Anne Frank,* and I remember one quote in particular about how children are responsible for their own upbringing. The accurate quote, when I looked online recently, is ". . . all children must look after their own upbringing. Parents can only give good advice and put them on the right paths, but the final forming of a person's character lies in their own hands."

I was fortunate that I was raised at a time and a place and by parents who were taught by their parents, and who thereafter taught me, to be blind to differences in gender, race, and color; that, given a good education, I am the equal of any man (if not better), and that if in a position to make a difference, I should make one.

Not everyone is as lucky as I am, with parents who believed in their children and ensured that we were all given a great education, both in school and at home— they "put me on the right path," as Anne Frank would say. I know that. The greatest lesson I learned from them, I believe, is that you learn from others and from your own experiences, strive for excellence in all things, and take responsibility for your own actions. When you fail, and you will (I certainly have had my share of failures), learn from them and move on. The final forming of your character does lie in your own hands. We are all fortunate that, given a good education, there are many paths to follow and many of them are, in fact, "right."

I will share one final quote. Gandhi said, "You must be the change you wish to see in the world." I emphasize: *be* the change.

RENAISSANCE PEOPLE

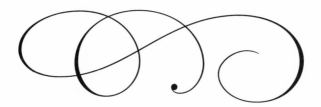

Giampiero Bodino

CREATIVE DIRECTOR, RICHEMONT

Giampiero Bodino not only designs the interiors of all the Dunhill showrooms worldwide, he also designs their new fashions, maintaining their trademark logo and making the Dunhill name an upscale, class brand worldwide. Here he gives us some great advice about investing our creative energy.

Giampiero Bodino has had an extensive career in the design industry, working with major luxury and fashion houses, including Bulgari, Gucci, Versace, and Swarovski. His association with the Richemont began in 1990. He has been involved in the design of watches, jewelry, accessories, and writing instruments. In February 2002 Bodino became creative director for Richemont and a key contributor to the Strategic Product and Communication Committee. He was subsequently appointed Cartier creative director, and in February 2004 he became group art director and a member of the Board of Richemont.

BE GENEROUS WITH YOUR CREATIVITY

My advice to young people who want to get to the top of the design world is this: Spend the same amount of energy on all the things you design, no matter how important the project is. So whether the product is small or is very important, be generous with your creativity. I think generosity is very important in all design work. So young people who get the chance to design something should do the best that they possibly can, no matter what they are designing. This is a simple rule, but I think it's very important.

John J. Brennan

How does a quiet, laid-back executive get to run one of the world's largest investment management companies? He just has fun controlling money and figuring out where to put it for maximum return. And he does pretty well! John J. Brennan's letter contains some valuable advice: Find an organization whose values match your own, and then enrich your experience within that organization by taking on a variety of assignments.

After earning an AB in economics at Dartmouth College, John J. Brennan began his career in 1976 as an associate at the New York Bank for Savings. After taking time to complete his MBA at Harvard Business School, he joined S. C. Johnson & Son as a planning associate. Two years later he moved to Vanguard, eventually becoming president in 1989, CEO in 1996, and chairman in 1998.

VALUES MATCH AND ADVENTUROUSNESS

The first thing to do is look for a values match: What's important to an organization, and what's important to you? That values match is the most important contributor to job satisfaction—which, in turn, leads to job success in my view. My other advice, which I tell people all the time, is to be adventuresome. Sometimes young people become too focused on trying to be X, Y, or Z. I don't think you can know that in advance. Every experience you have—interacting with clients, dealing with internal issues, working in finance, marketing, and so on—builds you as an individual as you move through your career. Therefore, if you're part of an organization you think very highly of, and you're asked to take on an assignment, do it. A quality organization will spend a huge amount of time to make you successful. To constrain your potential by being too narrowly focused is a huge mistake, and yet it's one I watch people make frequently.

Stefan Rojahn

CHAIRMAN OF THE BOARD OF
MANAGEMENT, WITTUR HOLDING GMBH

An excellent organizer with a German eye for detail,
Stefan Rojahn chooses greater and greater responsibilities and has been very successful in handling each one
of them. His advice tackles exactly that idea—taking on
increasing responsibilities is a key to achievement.

A graduate of the Technical University of Aachen (Germany) with a master's degree from California's San Jose
State University, Stefan Rojahn was appointed to the
board of RPC Group Plc in January 2006. He is chairman of the board of management of Wittur Holding
GmbH, a global supplier of elevator components. Between 2003 and 2005 he was chairman of the board of
management of Dürr AG. Previously he worked for more
than 20 years for the Bosch Group, leading to a position
on the board of management.

ASK FOR GREATER RESPONSIBILITIES

First of all, you have to get a good education. That includes speaking other languages, with English being customary for everyone in business today. Then I would recommend trying to get responsibility as soon as possible.

If you ask for greater responsibilities, you will probably forget about the job you are doing now. You have to do your job well, and then other people will recognize how you're doing. And if they are good leaders themselves, they will promote you to leadership positions. Everybody needs leaders.

Doreen A. Toben

EXECUTIVE VICE PRESIDENT AND CHIEF FINANCIAL OFFICER, VERIZON COMMUNICATIONS INC.

Doreen A. Toben is brilliant with figures, which is why she's also on the boards of the *New York Times* and JPMorgan Chase. She got to be very smart at an early age, and she explains how in this letter. It has to do with learning about all the component parts of your organization in order to best understand the inner workings and potential outcomes of strategy.

Doreen A. Toben is executive vice president and CFO for Verizon, a position she has held since April 2002. Prior to her current assignment, Toben was senior vice president and CFO for Verizon's domestic Telcom group. Toben began her career in 1983 at AT&T in treasury. In 2006 Toben was named one of the "50 Most Powerful Women in Business" by *Fortune* magazine; her fourth consecutive year on the list.

BROADEN YOUR OUTLOOK

There are all kinds of opportunities available for women in business, just as there are for men, if you are willing to put in the effort and take the right approach. You hear a lot about how success requires hard work and dedication—and that's true enough. But I'm also a firm believer that integrity and honesty are critical in achieving and maintaining success.

The best business advice I ever received was something I learned early in my career, and that was to try different parts of the business. I started out in finance and strategy, but then I managed field operations and took marketing jobs. I took jobs that helped me understand about technology and managing people. This broadened my outlook and brought to life all the numbers and all the strategy, and that made all the difference.

WORKING WITH OTHERS

Kathryn S. Wylde

PRESIDENT AND
CHIEF EXECUTIVE OFFICER,
NEW YORK CITY PARTNERSHIP

A close friend and adviser to almost every other
important name in New York City, Kathryn S. Wylde
has made partnering between companies and the
government essential to the health of the Big Apple
and its economy. And it's the idea of partnership
that she explores in her letter.

Kathryn S. Wylde is president and CEO of the Partnership for New York City, a nonprofit organization of the
city's business leaders established by David Rockefeller in
1979. The Partnership is dedicated to maintaining New
York City as a center of world commerce, finance, and innovation. She has played a major role in creating pioneering initiatives in affordable housing at the local, state, and
national levels. An internationally known expert in housing, economic development, and urban policy, Wylde
serves on a number of boards and advisory groups.

PARTNERSHIPS THAT CHANGE THE WORLD

As individuals most of us start out feeling powerless to make a difference in the world. We define the boundaries of what we hope to accomplish in life too narrowly, in terms of our own educational attainment, career ladder, and family aspirations. Those who are open to bigger dreams, however, soon find that one person can leave a legacy that is bigger than their own personal footprint. What does it take? Confidence in ourselves and our values. A clear vision of what we hope to accomplish. Trust in other people who share the vision and want to join together to pursue the same objectives. These are the qualities of leadership that allow each individual to leverage their small talents and energies in partnerships that change the world.

James S. Turley

A man of integrity leading a firm that is built on trust
and honesty, James S. Turley is a leader in the Boy Scouts
and a crusader for women's issues. In addition he is a
very good accountant. Turley offers us three important
qualities in good leaders and then closes with a fourth—
and it rhymes with *aptitude*.

James S. Turley is chairman and CEO of Ernst & Young,
a leading global professional services organization pro-
viding audit, risk advisory, tax, and transaction services.
Over the last twenty-eight years, Turley has held a series of leadership positions throughout Ernst & Young.
Throughout his career, he has actively supported numerous civic, cultural, and business organizations. He
is on the board of directors for Boy Scouts of America,
Catalyst, and the National Corporate Theater Fund. He
is also a member of the Business Roundtable and Trans-
atlantic Business Dialog.

INTEGRITY, RESPECT, AND TEAMING

Every now and then I am asked by our newest employees—people who have just graduated from universities—what advice I could give them as they begin their careers.

For me, this is one of the toughest questions to answer because we must all find our own paths to success. But no path will lead to success if we don't live our lives, both in our "work life" and our personal life, with a strong commitment to integrity, respect and teaming.

Integrity is the bedrock upon which all else is built. Without a solid foundation of integrity any success will ultimately crumble.

Respect of others is essential: those who think like you and those who don't; those who look like you and those who don't; those with whom you share common personal characteristics such as gender, race, nationality or sexual orientation and those with whom you have no such similarities. You will never earn the respect of others unless they feel your respect first. And any success one achieves in the absence of respect is shallow indeed.

And finally, a commitment to teaming is fundamental. No one succeeds for very long on his or her own. Virtually every successful person I have met—business leader, academic, politician, volunteer, parent, entrepreneur—has recognized that success is the product of our entire team working together for a common goal.

But at the end of the day, an important contributor to all three of these characteristics is a person's attitude. We all have different skills, different training, different aptitude. But attitude is much more important than aptitude. Be the kind of person who adds air and life to a room when they enter—not the kind who removes these things. The right attitude, and the right commitment to integrity, respect, and teaming, will take you a very long way.

Li Ka-shing

CHAIRMAN, CHEUNG KONG (HOLDINGS) LIMITED AND HUTCHISON WHAMPOA LIMITED

He's called the richest man in Asia and one of the largest landholders in China. Li Ka-shing is shrewd and knows almost everybody—and he knows them very well. He also knows that great advice often comes in a small package.

Li Ka-shing is chairman of Cheung Kong (Holdings) Limited and Hutchison Whampoa Limited. In 1950, he started Cheung Kong Industries. From manufacturing plastics, Li led and developed his company into a leading real estate investment company in Hong Kong. He continued to expand Cheung Kong by acquiring Hutchison Whampoa and Hongkong Electric Holdings Limited. *The Times* in the United Kingdom and Ernst & Young UK jointly named Li the "Entrepreneur of the Millennium" at the turn of the century. Li also founded Shantou University in 1981 in Shantou, China, to engineer reforms in China's education system.

FAIRNESS

Fairness and fair-mindedness—this is the win-win attitude for success in the business of life.

Charles O. Holliday Jr.

CHAIRMAN AND CHIEF EXECUTIVE OFFICER, DuPont

He spent his life in the chemical industry and is a mild-mannered worker behind the scenes. Charles O. Holliday Jr. shuns the spotlight but has built the giant DuPont into an even bigger giant. In his letter he makes it clear that getting things done and not clamoring for credit are keys to success.

A licensed professional engineer, Charles O. Holliday Jr. is the eighteenth executive in more than 200 years to lead DuPont. In 2004 he was elected a member of the National Academy of Engineering. He became chairman of the Business Roundtable's Task Force for Environment, Technology, and Economy the same year. Holliday is also past chairman of the World Business Council for Sustainable Development (WBCSD), the Business Council, and the Society of Chemical Industry—American Section.

NOT A BEAUTY CONTEST

Focus on determining what the most important work is for you, then set about achieving your goals. Make sure you deliver results. This is not a beauty contest, it is about delivering results, and you have to work toward that. Don't ever take the credit, and you should rarely let people give you the credit. You should give everybody else the credit, because people can see who gets what done.

I started out as a summer student at DuPont, and I thought that my whole DuPont career would be three months long. I thought it was wonderful, because I was making twice as much money as I had ever made before. I had an air-conditioned office. However, I didn't want a career with DuPont, because I thought I was going to work with my dad. I decided to get as much done as I possibly could in those three months. Every day was precious, and I had so much fun. So I had my three-month career, got a lot done, and had fun—and then I started over.

Maria Razumich-Zec

REGIONAL VICE PRESIDENT
AND GENERAL MANAGER,
THE PENINSULA HOTELS

There are only a limited number of women who run the world's finest hotels and who have earned the name "hotelier." The Peninsula in Chicago has one of the great experts, Maria Razumich-Zec, and she knows the hotel business in all its aspects better than most of her colleagues. As regional vice president and general manager for Peninsula Hotels, she's an unusual and delightful lady. The focus of her ten points of advice to us is our development of positive relationships with family, friends, and colleagues.

Maria Razumich-Zec assumed her current post with Peninsula Hotels in 2007, after serving as general manager of the Peninsula Chicago since 2002. Prior to joining the property, she served as managing director and then hotel manager at the New York Palace Hotel.

YOUR REPUTATION AND INTEGRITY ARE EVERYTHING

Throughout my life I have been inspired by my family, friends, and colleagues. The following are some of the principles that have guided me in my career and life:

1. Your reputation and integrity are everything. Follow through on what you say you're going to do. Your credibility can only be built over time, and it is built from the history of your words and actions.

2. Respond to people in a timely matter; this shows respect and responsibility.

3. Be nice and treat all individuals with respect, no matter what place or position they hold.

4. Take on additional responsibility wherever and whenever possible.

5. Dress and act for the position you aspire to have; soon others will see you in that role and the promotion will follow.

6. Approach situations with an open mind. Have no expectations, but rather abundant expectancy.

7. Listen to your gut. If something internally feels right or feels wrong to you, it probably is, so listen to your inner voice. Ask questions of yourself and be true to yourself. Know who you are and what you want, and let this mantra guide you through your life.

8. Have empathy for others. To have compassion is human and humbling.

9. It's important to give back to the community in which you live and work.

10. Attitude is EVERYTHING. Be positive, optimistic, engaging, spirited. You'll reap the rewards tenfold.

Farooq Kathwari

CHAIRMAN, PRESIDENT, AND CHIEF EXECUTIVE OFFICER, ETHAN ALLEN

Farooq Kathwari has built Ethan Allen into one of the largest furniture manufacturers in the world and into a brand that sells furniture for every purpose. He's originally from Kashmir and made it big in Big Town. Kathwari explains that leaders must practice and espouse the qualities and changes they want to see. And he gives us Ethan Allen's ten leadership principles.

Farooq Kathwari has been president of Ethan Allen Interiors Inc., since 1985 and chairman and CEO since 1988. In 1989 he formed a group to purchase Ethan Allen and took the company public in 1993. Under Kathwari's leadership Ethan Allen has been transformed into a leading vertically integrated interior design company. Kathwari serves on several not-for-profit organizations.

SHAPE THE DEBATE

I strongly believe that the responsibility of leadership is to shape the debate—to practice and project the right attributes—whether in a business enterprise, in our society, and even in our religions. If the leadership does not take the initiative of setting the priorities and the debate, the vacuum is filled often with dire consequences. The vacuum gets filled with people with louder voices and most extreme agendas, often with projections of hate, oppression, intolerance, injustice, and maintaining the status quo.

When I took charge of Ethan Allen in the mid-1980s, the company needed a major reinvention. The products were no longer relevant; the marketing and manufacturing needed a major overhaul. Management at the company was comfortable with the status quo and felt there was no need to change. A first major step in reinvention is that a core leadership group needs to be formed which accepts and embraces the need for change and helps in shaping the agenda and the debate for the rest of the organization. In the case of Ethan Allen, about sixteen years ago, I established a forty-member advisory group of our leaders known for their leadership quality, entrepreneurship, and respect by their peers. This group was key to helping transform Ethan Allen during the last fifteen years and has played a vital role in marketing the ideas and taking the leadership initiative for change. I also believe it is the responsibility of leadership to establish the overall environment and guidelines under which the enterprise will operate. In other words, every institution is defined by the culture that the leadership creates.

As we all know, much has been written about management and leadership principles. Years ago I felt the need to establish our "guidelines" or "instructions" to our leaders in conducting their affairs. We call them "Ethan Allen Leadership Principles," and they are available on our Web site, www.ethanalleninc.com.

The Ethan Allen Leadership Principles have helped us to create a unique culture which has developed a highly motivated leadership team which in time has helped us to inspire the 10,000 associates that we have. Our Leadership Principles focus on:

1. Leadership—Provide leadership by example
2. Accessibility—Be accessible, supportive, and recognize the contributions of others

3. Customer Focus—Understand that a leader's first responsibility is to the customer. Communicate this philosophy to all associates and encourage them to make customer service their first priority.
4. Excellence and Innovation—Have a passion for excellence and innovation
5. Self-confidence—Have the self-confidence to empower others to do their best
6. Change—Understand that change means opportunity and do not be afraid of it
7. Speed—Maintain a competitive advantage by reacting to new opportunities with speed
8. Hard Work—Establish a standard of hard work and practice it consistently
9. Prioritize—Establish priorities by clearly differentiating between the big issues and the small ones
10. Justice—Always make decisions fairly. Justice builds confidence and trust, which in turn encourages motivation and teamwork.

It is critically important for us that our leadership realize that the above principles are attributes of success for an individual and a business enterprise.

Bernd Pischetsrieder

FORMER CHAIRMAN, VOLKSWAGEN

An expert in the automotive field, Bernd Pischetsrieder helped build BMW and then went to Volkswagen and helped turn the company around into what is now the most profitable automobile company in Europe. He's Bavarian, so he's filled with charm and enthusiasm and loves what he does. According to Pischetsrieder, listening is always more important than talking, but true listening involves more than you may think.

―――――――――

Bernd Pischetsrieder is the only person ever to head two separate major car-manufacturing companies. He began his career with Bayerische Motoren Werke (BMW) and spent the first twenty years of his career designing, building, and assuring the quality of premium automobiles aimed at a wealthy public. After joining Volkswagen in 2000, the engineer-turned-manager began to change the image cultivated by decades of lowest-common-denominator "people's car" advertising. Pischetsrieder pushed for the introduction of luxury lines into a company that had made its reputation on building small cars for ordinary people.

LISTEN UP!

If there were one message I would give to young people, it would be that they often talk too much and do not listen enough. Of course, young people have their own opinions, but one doesn't learn by talking. One only learns by listening.

Listening is not just the physical action of hearing spoken words. One must also "listen" to the words of history, because much can be learned from history: societal history, business history, and philosophical history. The way people relate to each other rarely changes. The specific arguments and weapons might be different, but people are fundamentally the same as they were 1,000 years ago.

At the end of the day, education is more important than skills. People receive a lot of training and learn a lot of skills, but they lack the essential education to truly succeed as a member of this society. Education counts for more than skills in being a part of our society.

One always learns more from one's failures than from one's successes. Therefore, the earlier one makes a mistake and learns the lesson from that mistake, the more that person will benefit from that experience. I can't remember just one instance in which I have made a mistake, because there are just too many. However, I do know that the principal conflicts I have experienced have always had one simple cause: miscommunication. Either I didn't understand what other people wanted, or they didn't understand what I wanted. These conflicts were caused by a lack of communication and not just merely misunderstanding someone's words, but also misunderstanding a person's intentions and the background from which someone has formed an opinion. As such, my one piece of advice to young people is: Don't talk so much. Listen more.

CHAIRMAN AND CHIEF
EXECUTIVE OFFICER,
OGILVY & MATHER WORLDWIDE

The chief executive officer of one of the classiest and most important advertising agencies in the world, Shelly Lazarus still gets personally involved in the work at every level. She also advises the chief executive officers of American Express and IBM, in addition to many others, who use her ideas to help make their companies even more successful. In her letter Lazarus explains how leadership can be defined as having the courage to be yourself.

Shelly Lazarus joined Ogilvy & Mather Worldwide, a multinational advertising agency, in 1971, becoming president of its U.S. direct marketing business in 1989. She then became president of Ogilvy & Mather New York and president of Ogilvy & Mather North America before becoming president and COO of the worldwide agency in 1995, CEO in 1996, and chairman in 1997.

"I'D RATHER ASK FOR FORGIVENESS THAN PERMISSION."

I have often been invited to speak about the topic of leadership. The only real authority I bring to the subject is experience. One of the great things about my job is that I get to observe leaders across a wide range of organizations. And from over thirty years of observing, the first thing I would tell you is that there is no one way of leading, no magic formula, no sure-fire list of "to dos."

I would suggest to you that leadership is an individual pursuit. And what that individual route demands is the courage to be yourself. Leadership demands the courage to speak up; to ask hard questions; to say "no." Leaders don't just go with the flow. They are not necessarily polite (although there is always a "nice way" to say anything, I have found). They are not afraid to say what they think and do what they think is right, even when it goes counter to conventional thinking or "orders" received from management. One of my favorite lines is, "I'd rather ask for forgiveness than permission." This is not easy . . . but definitely in your control.

Leaders tend to be passionate about what they do. I urge you to do whatever it takes to get yourself in a position where you love what you do, where you care about what you do, where you want to inspire others, build great things, do great deeds. Only then will you find true fulfillment. Only then will you be a brilliant leader.

Sanford I. Weill

CHAIRMAN EMERITUS, CITIGROUP INC., NEW YORK

Sanford I. Weill built many conglomerates, but the biggest is Citigroup. Now he devotes his life to his wife and good causes like the Weill Pavilion at New York Hospital. He's put his billions to good work for others. In his open letter to our future leaders, Weill discusses a variety of issues, including the idea of "surfacing" one's mistakes and teaming with others to correct them.

Sanford I. Weill is chairman emeritus of Citigroup Inc., having retired as CEO in 2003, and as chairman in 2006. Most recently President Bush asked Weill to join four other private-sector business leaders in heading up a nationwide effort to encourage private donations for relief and reconstruction in response to the October 8, 2005, South Asia earthquake.

SURFACE THAT MISTAKE

My advice to young people would start with recommending that they not be in too much of a hurry and that they make sure that they have a good grounding in the basics. Also, have a little diversity of interest. By that I mean, don't just be interested in the commercial side of what they're doing. Instead, think a little bit about what they're learning while they're on their full-time job that can also be utilized to get them involved, at an early age, in a not-for-profit area that helps make our world a better place.

Even before they are very successful and have a lot of money, they can still be very philanthropic by giving of their time and their abilities and by developing a passion to care about the community and the world that they live in. They should get involved in an organization that is active in an area that they're interested in—whether that's the social services area or the arts or medicine or something else—and volunteer their time in that enterprise, because most of the not-for-profit organizations in the world really have a dearth of talent and need contributions of talent from the for-profit side. This will also help them in their careers.

To achieve their goals, they should always keep throwing the rope out a little bit further toward a goal that is understandable and achievable, and when they get near that goal, throw the rope out a little further. Believe that through hard work they can make a lot of good things happen.

They should also be well prepared for opportunities that might arise. In my field I read a lot about the financial industry—maybe just about everything that was written on it. I read about companies that I respected and thought were doing well, and I tried to understand why they were doing well. I always looked at an environment of change—but as an opportunity rather than something to fear. When things do change, the greatest opportunities are presented to those who understand what that change means before others.

In dealing with adversity, they should never really focus very long on people not treating them right. Lots of things that they hope will happen, won't happen. Develop the ability to rationalize that way in the background and believe that a better opportunity is going to be around the corner if they keep on working.

Try to wake up every morning happy. They may not go to bed every night happy, but the next morning, be happy and enthusiastic again. If they want to be a leader, they should realize that people like following and working with people who are enthusiastic, who have energy, who have a passion for what they do, and who are somewhat realistic in their enthusiasm.

So first, learn the basics. Second, be a team player. I think those are the two most important things. Third, don't be greedy. If they do the right thing, usually the rewards follow. Fourth, create a balance to their lives, both with their families and with their contributions to society outside of what they do in business. Finally, realize that mistakes are okay. If they do make a mistake, surface that mistake and don't try and resolve it all by themselves. Admit what happened and get the best help they can to resolve the situation. Most good companies recognize that nobody's perfect and that people are going to make mistakes. Nobody will make any great decisions unless they are in an environment where they can make mistakes. But they surface that mistake.

Beth Brooke

GLOBAL VICE CHAIR, ERNST & YOUNG

Beth Brooke was a star collegiate athlete and credits the discipline of sports teamwork for her success. She's global vice chair of one of the largest accounting firms in the world, which goes to show there's much to be gained from competitive sports. Her advice is about using your platform, that unique perspective each one of us has and from which we can make our own difference in this world.

Prior to assuming her current position in 2003, Beth Brooke served as national director of tax consulting services for Ernst & Young in the United States. She temporarily left Ernst & Young in 1993 to join the Clinton Administration, where she was responsible for all tax-policy matters related to insurance and managed care. Brooke also serves on the boards of the Partnership for Public Service, the White House Project, the Atlantic Council of the United States, Technoserve, the Committee for Economic Development, and the National Women's Hall of Fame Advisory Council.

USE YOUR PLATFORM

One of the most important things you can do, regardless of where you are in life, is to make a difference in
the world. Every one of us has a platform. It may be the
job you have; it may be your role in your community
or even in your family. It changes over time and looks
different for every individual, but we all have one. Use
your platform— however large or small—to make a difference. Speak up when a voice is needed. Reach out
to those in need. Strive every day to be invaluable to
others.

As you navigate through life, listen and be responsive
to the world around you. Focus on others. Be open to
different perspectives. Other people may have ideas,
and often times you may have resources. Lives are for-
ever changed and great things accomplished when you
look for ways to make a difference. Whatever path your
life takes, go where you can make a difference.

WORKING *FOR* OTHERS

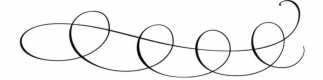

Richard Holbrooke

He almost became secretary of state and may still.
During his time as an ambassador to the United
Nations, he was a great conciliator between hostile
nations and the United States Senate and the secretary
general. Richard Holbrooke is exceptionally knowledgeable in foreign affairs as it affects Asia. Citing JFK's
inaugural call to the nation, he describes the role we
all must play in the public sphere.

———————

Vice chairman of Perseus, Richard Holbrooke served as
the U.S. ambassador to the United Nations, where he was
also a member of President Clinton's cabinet (1999–2001).
He was assistant secretary of state for Europe (1994–1996),
and later served as President Clinton's special envoy to
Bosnia and Kosovo and special envoy to Cyprus. From
1993 to 1994 Holbrooke was the U.S. ambassador to Germany. During the Carter Administration (1977–1981), he
was assistant secretary of state for East Asian and Pacific
Affairs and was in charge of U.S. relations with China.

TO PUBLIC SERVICE

I entered government as a direct result of President Kennedy's inaugural call: Ask not what your country can do for you, but what you can do for your country. In those days, that wasn't a sound bite or a cliché. It was a real, live call to action. So I entered the Foreign Service, inspired by Kennedy, and thinking that people could make a difference. I still believe that is true, as frustrating as government service can be. I believe that every person should try to give part of his or her life to public service, whether in government or through local community organizations or nongovernmental organizations. Whether people are liberal or conservative, Republican or Democrat, they should try to do something beyond their family lives and their professional lives. People should give back to society, if they can. I speak particularly to those Americans who are fortunate enough to have some degree of financial comfort. They are the ones who should give back the most.

John D. Negroponte

DEPUTY SECRETARY OF STATE, UNITED STATES

I first met John D. Negroponte when he was ambassador to the Philippines, and he's worked his way up to become ambassador to the United Nations and now deputy secretary of state. He is one of the most knowledgeable figures in the United States regarding foreign affairs and government. In his letter Negroponte expounds on the many benefits of a life in the service of the common good.

———

From February 13, 2007, to the end of the Bush Administration, John D. Negroponte was the deputy secretary of state. Prior to this assignment, Negroponte served as the first director of national intelligence (2005–2007), U.S. ambassador to Iraq (2004–2005), and U.S. representative to the United Nations (2001–2004).

Among his prior assignments, Negroponte was ambassador to Honduras; deputy assistant secretary of state for Oceans and Fisheries and then for the Bureau of East Asian and Pacific Affairs; national security adviser under Reagan; ambassador to Mexico; and ambassador to the Philippines.

A LIFE IN PUBLIC SERVICE

Everyone has to make up his or her own mind, but I would think that 9/11 would drive more and more young people into public service, rather than keep them out. A career in public service has enabled me to live and work on four continents, study several languages, contribute to issues as diverse as rural development in Africa and helping democracy take root in Central America, and wake up every morning knowing that the issues that preoccupy me are the issues that preoccupy the world. A life in public service is bigger than the public servant—I'll tell you that. I would not have traded my time in government for any other career.

Diana DeGette

As a leading legislator on public policy for ethical,
cutting-edge scientific research and as a Congressional
whip, Diana DeGette knows the dedication it takes to
be successful in public service and how rewarding it can
be. During more than fifteen years in office, she has
worked to improve our lives. In her letter she explains
the benefits of a career in government.

Diana DeGette is in her sixth term in Congress as the
representative of the First Congressional District of Colorado. DeGette serves in the House leadership as chief
deputy whip and is cochair of both the bipartisan Pro-
Choice Caucus and the Congressional Diabetes Caucus.
In 2007 she was appointed vice chair of the Committee
on Energy and Commerce, which has wide jurisdiction
over health care, trade, technology, consumer protection, and food safety policy in Congress. She is also the
chief architect of the Stem Cell Research Enhancement
Act, which passed both the House and Senate.

THE BENEFIT OF CHANGING LIVES

As a girl I wanted to be a lawyer, because I saw it as a way to help people. I went to law school and became a public-interest lawyer helping people solve their legal problems.

After many years of practicing law, I realized that I could have a bigger impact on people's lives if I could *write* the laws that would affect them. So I ran for the Colorado legislature and was elected. I found that I *was* able to positively contribute. After four years I had an opportunity to run for the U.S. Congress. I was elected, and am finishing my sixth term.

I can tell you that, based on my experience, there is no better way to affect lives for the better. I have focused on social equality, improving health care, promoting medical research, and protecting the environment.

Whatever your interest is—whether science, public health, military affairs, or the environment—you can immerse yourself and have a fulfilling career that also has the benefit of changing lives. Best of luck. *You* are our future leaders.

His Majesty
King Bhumibol Adulyadej

KING OF THAILAND

King Bhumibol Adulyadej exhibits an appropriately distinguished and "kingly" public façade, yet he remains a down-to-earth, warm, and kindly private individual—a devout Buddhist who also appreciates jazz and making short-wave radio contact with those unaware of his true identity. He sees himself not as the exalted apex of the social pyramid, but rather as its base, believing that it is his responsibility to support the population's welfare. In his message he suggests that anyone who dreams of being a leader should hold on to a similar belief.

His Majesty the King attended the Ecole Nouvelle de la Suisse Romande, Chailly sur Lausanne, and later the Gymnase Classique Cantonal of Lausanne where he received his *bachelier es lettres* diploma. After the sudden death of his elder brother, King Ananda Mahidol, in 1946, the Law of Succession bestowed on him the Thai Crown. His Majesty went back to Switzerland to study political science and law to prepare himself for government. He completed his education in the early 1950s and returned home to Thailand.

THE PURE SOUL

[Anyone aspiring to be a leader must remember that] the phrase "to be human" is everything, and nothing. One must be human. This means that one must know that everything which one does as Head of State, or as soldiers, or as interviewers, or as photographers, must have a reason. One must always be human, but at the same time one may be inhuman. To be human is important, but one must also be inhuman when one is in this position, or in any high position. One must do work in superhuman ways. One must do it. One must make the things that are best for the nation or fellow humans. If we do things that are best for fellow humans, then it will be better for us, since we have achieved something. We are here to be human, to make money so that we have money to spend, and to make a good name for ourselves so that we are praised. But all this, if we have money, we will spend it, and in the end we will lose the money. What is left is the pure soul. That is what we must attain—the pure soul. But if we are to attain the pure soul, we must give. Giving of the heart and the feeling is one reason why leaders, if they are in a high position, should not think that their high position has been earned by hard work alone. Yes, it has been earned by hard work. But not only that: The position has to be maintained. This will lead to a more satisfying feeling for the soul. That is the reason why the leaders of the world should do that—they should give more and take less.

CLAIMING YOUR PLACE IN THE WORLD

Lord E. John P. Browne

A gentle but strong-willed executive titan who built
British Petroleum (BP) into a major world brand,
Lord E. John P. Browne expanded the company from
energy producer to an organization dedicated to the
environmental health of planet Earth. In his letter he
suggests that you create areas of expertise by becoming
excellent at one thing at a time and learning how to
bounce back from failure.

Lord E. John P. Browne began working for BP in Alaska's
Prudhoe Bay as an engineer on a pipeline. By 1989 BP
was the largest petroleum producer in the United States,
and in 1995 Browne was made CEO, for helping to sta-
bilize the company. In a 1997 speech at Stanford University, Browne declared that evidence suggested that global
warming could be real, and he soon made the term *green*
a fundamental part of BP's operations. Not only commit-
ting BP to producing cleaner fuels and cleaning up its
production waste, Browne brought BP into the business of
creating alternative sources of energy.

BUILD A STRONG CORE

My first advice to anyone is to become really good at one thing. Don't try to ascend to generality before you've become fabulously successful at one undertaking. Build a strong core, whatever you're doing. And in doing so, make sure to establish principles against which to measure yourself.

Mastering one thing seems to me to be the single most important career move, yet it's very difficult to persuade people to do so. I continually look at people at BP and say, for example: "Become a great petroleum engineer first, and don't give up halfway through. After you've done that, do something else." Or: "You've joined us as a comptroller. Become a great comptroller first. Then after you've done that, you can apply your expertise in other directions." You can't build on nothing; you need a core. That's the bit of career advice I give to absolutely everybody.

Whether a situation is personal or business related, you have to have certain standards and values you believe in, which you can rely upon when everything around you isn't going well. Personally, I have the determined belief that the best is yet to come. I believe very firmly in that. If I didn't believe it, I'd have to stop going forward.

In the case of failure, what do you do to make things better? The answer isn't to go backward and perhaps avoid all risk in the future. Rather, the answer is to say: "Okay. This is the situation. I'm going to figure out how to remedy matters, because the best is yet to come." I was very close to my late mother, who died four years ago and was my best friend. Her death affected me greatly. But I decided that, if the best is yet to come, then I should make sure that my closest friends were secured to serve as a surrogate family. And that's just what I did. I didn't say: "Woe is me. What am I going to do?" I took a very firm and positive approach to meet the future.

Tony Hall

CHIEF EXECUTIVE OFFICER, THE ROYAL OPERA HOUSE, LONDON

Tony Hall holds the dual role of running the Royal Opera House in London and raising funds to continue making the Royal Opera House one of the finest in the world. Previously in the television/news business, his contacts have proven valuable in helping all kinds of music stay alive in London and the United Kingdom.

Here he suggests that by engaging in different experiences—testing things out—you will learn what role you can play successfully within your desired field.

Tony Hall joined the Royal Opera House from the BBC, where he had been director of BBC News, the biggest news organization in the world. After joining the Royal Opera House, Hall set up ROH2, a department devoted to supporting new artists and developing new audiences. Since then, Hall has set up new initiatives to widen access to the Opera House.

MANY DIFFERENT ROLES

See what work and what experience you can get. At college or university, play and try things out to see what you're good at. Many people love opera and ballet, but find out that, unfortunately, they will not be a singer or a dancer. However, there are many different roles they can fill to contribute toward those art forms. And you will only discover those roles and discover where your real talent lies by working in these areas and learning about them. Don't give up.

Thomas Hoving

A legend in the field of art, Thomas Hoving is nobody's
fool and has always said exactly what he means, like
it or not. Now he is considered the grand old man of
art, probably the world's greatest expert on medieval
works. Although specific to the art world, Hoving's
letter contains sage advice on looking within any field
for a role that is in great demand.

———————

Thomas Hoving, former director of the Metropolitan
Museum of Art, also served as editor of *Connossieur* and
cultural correspondent for ABC's *20/20*. The author of
fifteen books, including the bestsellers *Making the Mum-
mies Dance* and *Tutankhamun, the Untold Story,* he lives in
New York City.

EVERYBODY WANTS YOU

When I was a kid about to enter graduate school, I asked, "What do I need to be a professional in art history?" A professor replied, "Independent income." And that probably still is a factor. If I were to do it again, I would not go into art history. I would go into conservation. Everybody wants you. It's extraordinarily exciting. Everybody wants things fixed or repaired or kept up for history. You'll never not have a job. The excitement of discovery is intense, and the field is not all that crowded yet. I would go into conservation, just like that!

Donald R. Keough

He is probably one of the most influential business leaders in America. Responsible along with Roberto Goizueta for the great success of Coca-Cola, Donald R. Keough was instrumental in the acquisition of Columbia Pictures and countless other business deals. He's an Irishman with a twinkle in his eye, a great sense of humor, and so many friends he can't count them. In anecdotal form, Keough illustrates how the decision over how to invest one's energy can have profound effects.

For more than five years Donald R. Keough has been nonexecutive chairman of the board of Allen & Company Incorporated, a privately held investment firm, and nonexecutive chairman of the board of Allen & Company LLC, an investment-banking firm. He is also a director of the Coca-Cola Company, Berkshire Hathaway Inc., Convera Corporation, and IAC/InterActiveCorp.

A LITTLE DECISION

Life has those special moments that at the time seem relatively unimportant but prove to be highly significant.

My life took a totally different direction because my mother encouraged me to rethink a little decision at age fourteen.

In the orientation session on my first day as a high school freshman in Sioux City, Iowa, I was given the opportunity to decide what extracurricular activity interested me. There was a long list of possibilities from which to choose. I signed up for tumbling (jumping on a trampoline). When I came home that day, my mother looked over the list and asked what activity I had chosen. "Tumbling," I replied. My mother looked over the list, raised her eyes, and said, "Do you want to spend much of your life jumping up and down?" I replied, "No, Mother." She said, "You are right, let's choose debating," and I did.

The rest of my life I have done very little jumping and a lot of debating. Thanks, Mother!

David Rockefeller Jr.

MEMBER OF THE BOARD,
ROCKEFELLER FINANCIAL SERVICES

David Rockefeller Jr.'s father was chairman of the Chase Bank. As the surviving son among five Rockefeller brothers, his father is carrying on the family tradition, not only in investing the Rockefeller finances, but also in the family's charitable causes, which are immense and not often publicized. Following his first piece of advice about finding your true interests, Rockefeller Jr. gives us some keys to leading fulfilling lives.

David Rockefeller Jr., is a director and former chairman of Rockefeller & Co., and has been an active participant in the areas of environment, philanthropy, arts, and public education. Rockefeller is vice chair emeritus of the National Park Foundation; the former chair of the North American Nominating Committee for the Praemium Imperiale, the Japanese prize for outstanding international achievement in the arts; a trustee of the Museum of Modern Art and the Asian Cultural Council; and a fellow of the American Academy of Arts and Sciences.

DIG IN

First, find out what really interests you in life, and then dig in and discover a lot about it. Become an expert or, at least, become very well informed. As much as it is economically possible, follow the things you really care about in life and work with people you like. Try to craft a career or a life path that is meaningful, and then the energy will flow naturally. If you only do the things you think you ought to do, it will always be a struggle to get up in the morning. However, if you have a great project that you love—whether it's your garden, your children, your business, or your sport—you won't have trouble getting up. So follow your passion. Go deep, work hard, and always be open to learning. The world is so interesting and so full of information about people, nature, and the mechanics of things. Never stop learning.

Also, remember that we all get down sometimes, so make good friends, because friends support you and they probably won't be down when you are. Don't be shy about going to them for support, and they'll also come to you.

Sir David Tang

CHAIRMAN AND MANAGING DIRECTOR, D.W.C. TANG DEVELOPMENT LIMITED

Sir David Tang is a leader in many fields, and even talked Fidel Castro into giving him the cigar concession for all of Asia. He's known as one of the most personable and charming characters in Hong Kong and has a Rolodex of friends almost comparable to David Rockefeller Sr.'s. No matter the course you take in life, according to Tang, you should strive to excel in a certain niche. Become *the* leader in that realm.

Born in Hong Kong, Sir David Tang received his education in Hong Kong, Cambridge, London, and Beijing. In addition to his responsibilities at D.W.C. Tang Development, he is the founder and chairman of the China Clubs in Hong Kong, Peking, Singapore, and London; the Shanghai Tang Department Stores; and the Pacific Cigar Co. He was made an Officer of the British Empire in 1997 and Chevalier de L'Ordre des Arts et des Lettres (France) in 1995.

A KING IN EVERY JOB

The best advice I can give anyone young is that they must always remain focused and they must just get on with whatever they want to do and do it well. It is important to excel in whatever you do, however lowly the job. There is a Chinese saying: "There is a king in every job." The secret is that being the king in one job makes it easier for you to become a king in another job. And never kid yourself that just because you are determined, good with people, good at analysis, diligent, sensible, responsible, and hard-working, you are qualified to be employed. These are merely the minimum requirements. You should always look for a niche—somewhere others have not been or something others have not done. And most important of all, stop talking and make a start.

James S. Tisch

Loews Corporation owns hotels, sports teams, and watch companies, and James S. Tisch oversees them all. He is a juggling genius with some great advice about roads less traveled. Just because it seems that the most remunerative jobs are in a certain sector of the economy, such as Wall Street, does not mean you should jump into that particular fray. As Tisch writes, and as he *lives* in his role as the head of Loews, all businesses and organizations are interdependent, and your chance at success may be somewhere off the beaten path.

James S. Tisch has been with Loews Corporation since 1977, serving as a director since 1986, president since 1994, and CEO since January 1999. He is also chairman of the board of Diamond Offshore Drilling Inc. Tisch serves as chairman of the board of Educational Broadcasting Corporation and he serves on the board of directors of CNA Financial Corporation.

GO AGAINST THE GRAIN

I would advise the leaders of tomorrow that there are lots of businesses out there that need really good, smart managers. In my view that requires people to go against the grain—to do what everybody else isn't doing. As I said, right now the best and the brightest are going into Wall Street and hedge funds. But I tell young people, "If you're talented and ambitious, go elsewhere, because then it will be easier to get ahead." It is important to remember that those Wall Street paper and money shufflers actually have to shuffle something, and what they shuffle are American businesses. We need good, high-quality people to run and grow those businesses. So I say, "If you're one of those people, your value will be seen and you will, I think, have a more fulfilling and remunerative career in business than you would have had on Wall Street."

FOCUS/DEDICATION

Henry Kaufman

PRESIDENT,
HENRY KAUFMAN & COMPANY, INC.

Henry Kaufman was thought of as "Dr. Gloom" when he was an adviser to Wall Street. He's still an adviser and still sought after to predict the future of the economy, and it's amazing how right he usually is. In his letter he suggests that even if it takes ten-hour days of study or twelve-hour workdays, you must follow through completely to achieve success.

———————

Henry Kaufman has been president of Henry Kaufman & Company, Inc., an investment management and economic and financial consulting firm, since 1988. For the previous twenty-six years, he was with Salomon Brothers Inc., where he was a managing director, member of the Executive Committee, and in charge of Salomon's four research departments. He was also a vice chairman of the parent company, Salomon Inc.

PERSISTENCE

It was very difficult when I was growing up, but I was very fortunate. First of all, there has to be a willingness to persist and to work toward where you want to go and what you want to do, and you have to set up priorities early on, as you're moving from the university life to business life. Persistence is a very critical issue, and if it means studying ten hours a day, it means studying ten hours a day. If it means working twelve hours a day, it means working twelve hours a day. That really is number one. Also, of course, it goes without saying that you should get as strong an education as you possibly can. That's very important in this environment. Next, in terms of craftsmanship, learn how to verbalize and learn how to write reasonably well, because we sell ourselves by speaking, and to me that is probably more important than writing, although we also learn how to express ourselves in writing. Knowing how to verbalize is critical. I can't stress that enough, particularly for people who graduate with MBA degrees and so on. Next, I think you would be very fortunate to find someone who will give you objective advice as you move along in your career. I know all of these things have helped me over time.

Raymond W. Kelly

COMMISSIONER,
NEW YORK CITY POLICE DEPARTMENT

Some say Raymond W. Kelly is the best police
commissioner New York City has had in the last fifty
years. Mayor Bloomberg says so, and Kelly is completely
devoted to his cops and to serving the public. Some even
think he would make a great mayor. A former marine,
Kelly gives us the principles he learned in the Corps,
principles that lead visionaries to success.

Raymond W. Kelly is the first person to serve as commissioner of the New York City Police Department for
two separate tenures. He was formerly senior managing
director of global corporate security at Bear, Stearns &
Co. Inc. Before that he served as commissioner of the
U.S. Customs Service. From 1996 to 1998, he was under-
secretary for enforcement at the U.S. Treasury Department. Kelly spent thirty-one years in the New York City
Police Department, serving in twenty-five different com-
mands. A combat veteran of the Vietnam War, he retired
as a colonel from the Marine Corps Reserves after thirty
years of service.

DEVOTE YOURSELF TOTALLY

Just about everything I have learned about leadership I learned in the Marine Corps. At a fairly young age I learned a few basic tenets and principles that I use every day.

You need to have a certain amount of discipline and knowledge about your job. So focus on your job and learn it well. I also think it's necessary to have integrity and enthusiasm. If you don't like what you're doing, you might never succeed and you're certainly not going to be happy. If you find something you like doing, you'll do it well.

I have given a couple of graduation speeches, and I always say that money is overrated. I've never made a decision based on money, and I've never regretted it. So don't make a decision based on money. America has enough moneymakers. We need visionaries and people with principles. It's nice to have money, but if it's your sole motivation, you're missing something.

So my advice to young people is: Feel your way around, find something you really like doing, and devote yourself to it totally. That course of action will lead to success.

Leon M. Lederman

You have to be a genius of some kind to get a Nobel
Prize, and Leon M. Lederman has that title. He also
has one of the greatest heads of hair among all Nobel
laureates. Yet, neither great hair nor talent alone,
he explains, leads to success.

Leon M. Lederman earned his master's and Ph.D. in
physics at Columbia University. Lederman remained at
Columbia following his studies for nearly thirty years. In
1963 he proposed the idea that eventually became the Fer-
mi National Accelerator Laboratory in Batavia, Illinois.
The 1988 Nobel Prize in Physics was awarded to Lederman and his old partners, Melvin Schwartz and Jack
Steinberger for "transforming the ghostly neutrino into an
active tool of research." In 1989 Lederman stepped down
as director of Fermilab and assumed the title "director
emeritus." Today he is Pritzker Professor of Physics at the
Illinois Institute of Technology.

TOTAL OBSESSIVE DEDICATION

My greatest challenge was to succeed in my chosen profession and passion of research in physics given limited intellectual capabilities.

This is not at all modesty or humility. It is a clean recognition, verified by the mediocre grades received in middle, high school, and college and seconded by intimate contact with creative physicists as teachers and colleagues. One would not expect a B (sometimes B+) student to make important discoveries in elementary particle physics.

The process of "overcoming" such a formidable handicap involved much hard work, total obsessive dedication, luck, and a few sparks of imagination.

Dean Kamen

PRESIDENT, DEKA RESEARCH

Dean Kamen is an inventor with a wry personality that, I suppose, most inventors must have. Some call him a genius, and some say he's a little hard to get along with. He's probably both. Here he gives us some tough-love advice about what to do with one's time.

Dean Kamen is the president of DEKA Research & Development Corporation. As an inventor, physicist, and entrepreneur, he has dedicated his life to developing technologies that help people lead better lives. Some of his notable breakthrough medical devices include the HomeChoice® portable dialysis machine, marketed by Baxter Healthcare, and the Independence® IBOT® 4000 Mobility System, a sophisticated mobility aid developed for Johnson & Johnson. Kamen is also widely recognized as the inventor of the Segway® Human Transporter. He is a member of the National Academy of Engineering and was inducted into the National Inventors Hall of Fame in 2005.

YOU MAKE THE CHOICE

Figure out what's important to you. Adults can help you do that, because presumably adults have good judgment to determine what is important and what is not important, what is true and what is false, what is a worthy pursuit and what is a mere distraction. Society owes kids a road map that shows them what is important.

That said, learning is a very personal thing. You have to learn by working, reading, rereading, and sweating. You can watch football or basketball all day, but the only way you'll get better at a sport is by working at it. Likewise, the only way your mind will improve is if you work at it. Nobody else can do that for you, and nobody else can be blamed if you don't work hard enough to achieve that. I would tell kids this cold, hard reality: You can't blame your parents, teachers, or government for anything. Don't look in the mirror and whine. You either make the choice to spend each day wisely, preparing yourself for the future, or you don't. Every American kid has access to books. So you don't have a computer! So you don't have other tools! Spare me!

Success is hard to achieve, and it can be frustrating, but it's worth it.

Ultimately you make the choice, and in the end, you either pay for your choices or reap the rewards of your choices. When I visit schools I tell kids that's what's great about America: You make the choice. You can have a good time, but if you do that at the expense of your future, you'll pay for it. It's your choice. Of course, certain pastimes are fun, and kids should spend time playing sports or entertaining themselves otherwise. These are things that are important to us, our culture, our countries, and our world. If you can't have a little fun, you won't have much of a life and the world could end up being a pretty unpleasant place.

Richard S. LeFrak

**CHAIRMAN, PRESIDENT,
AND CHIEF EXECUTIVE OFFICER,
LEFRAK ORGANIZATION**

Richard S. LeFrak has spent a lifetime in the real estate business. The LeFrak Organization owns so many buildings in all the boroughs of New York City, that he is known as "the most successful quiet landlord." You may read and hear a lot about Donald Trump, but LeFrak resides behind the curtain, bringing in tons of money. In his letter LeFrak discusses epiphanies, how so few of us are blessed with wholly original ones, and how most of us therefore achieve success through complete dedication to our goals.

Richard S. LeFrak is president, chairman, and CEO of LeFrak Organization, which his grandfather founded in 1901. The Organization is active in major residential and commercial real estate development, oil and gas exploration, and financial investments.

FOR LACK OF AN EPIPHANY

I think Woody Allen put a line in one of his movies that said, "You know, 90 percent of life is just showing up." I like to recall that phrase when talking about people's careers and their work ethics, because most of us are not blessed with having an epiphany. Some of us do have the creativity to be original, but with most of us, it's just about how much effort we put into what we do. And therefore my advice is stay focused on your objectives, whatever they may be. Stick with your objectives—that always seems to be a very good formula for achieving your goals.

The world that twenty-year-olds today are coming into is far more complicated and difficult than the world I came into. They're coming into a global society, a global economy, a global marketplace—and they're not competing with the person next door; they're competing with the world. Therefore they have to be just that much better, because the global community is now the best and the brightest it has ever been. The competition isn't just in the United States. It's in the United States,

Europe, Asia—in fact, it's all over this planet. So you've got to be that much better than we were to succeed. On the other hand, the digital age is giving everyone tremendous opportunities and new ways of communicating. That is all wonderful stuff.

Gary Mirabelle

Gary Mirabelle gained fame by sculpting life-size
figures dressed in real clothes. They are startling. Now
he has branched out into a series of bronze miniatures,
and he's begun taking photographs that are as awe-
inspiring as his sculptures. In his letter Mirabelle
explains how art can be so very unrewarding financially.
But if it's a labor of love, and you dedicate yourself to
it fully, the benefits of that labor will come. And that's
some wisdom that applies to any field.

After formal art training, Gary Mirabelle modeled toy
prototypes from clay and worked as a head sculptor for
an architectural restoration firm. On the side, he produced realistic special effects for low-budget feature films.
Mirabelle's work has been labeled as photo-realism or
even hyperrealism. Yet it is his emotional insights and
wry, satirical wit that sets his work apart from others.
Mirabelle's sculptures are modeled from clay, then cast
in resin. Working as a full-time sculptor in his Tribeca
studio fulfills his lifelong dream.

ABSURDLY DEDICATED

I would advise any young person that, if you think you're going to make any money in the fine arts, the odds are stacked against you. You're probably going to have to support yourself with a different kind of job. I was fortunate enough to work as a sculptor for other people for years. And then was able to make some connections, and make the transition to being a fine artist on my own. But you need an element of luck and good timing. You have to develop your skills and you have to be absurdly dedicated to it. A lot of times there is a great cost involved. I did not really start making any money as an artist until I was forty years old. That was a long time to wait, even though I had a lot of education. In any other field, I probably would have been off and running by then with a good income. So you have to really love it. The money almost has to be a secondary part of why you do it. If it comes, great. But if it doesn't, it has to be a labor of love.

I would strongly recommend that you get good training. You don't have to, but I think to get your foundation established, a good art education is very valid. After you are trained, you can go to work for another artist or work in a business where your skills as an artist will be tapped. Obviously, if you want to come out as a painter, you don't want to go work in a normal business office. But if you can go to work as a graphic artist for a magazine or as something where your skills are at least being tapped into, I think that's more of the way to go. Try to keep it as related to your field as you can, then keep pushing.

Your goal is to get into the galleries. Put your work together. It takes a long time to put a body of work together. You've got to be unique. You have to stand out, and you have to push. You have to be aggressive. There are artists out there who do it on sheer, incredible, awesome talent, and there are other artists who make it on sheer hustle. Some people are brilliant at promoting themselves. That's their skill, and they can create a niche and just go with it. A lot of contemporary artists do that now. Some are just incredibly good. You see their work and get blown away by it.

You may have runs where you're not selling well. You may lose some galleries. You may lose some commissions. But it's always about the work. The work is always there. Just turn and create some more art. That's really what it's about. Even before I had my own studio, when I was young, it was always about going into a room—even if it were a bedroom in my apartment—and putting out stuff. I was always thinking and dreaming about what I wanted to sculpt. So it's always about the artwork. And there's always a way to do it. Work within your realm, with what you have. If you can't afford a big space, then work in a small space.

Also, always follow your real interests. From the beginning I always developed myself as a classical artist, but I always loved doing humorous sculpture. I guess it's just part of the pop culture I grew up in. In the early 1990s, I saw artists like Red Grooms, who created comic realism, and Dwayne Hanson, who created hyperrealism. I loved their work and knew it was still a wide-open field back then. I saw this niche that I could develop in life-size figures that nobody was doing. My work was in between those two artists—a sort of a hyperrealistic, sculpted piece as opposed to a body cast, but not quite as cartoony as a Red Grooms. This was a whole middle ground that had yet to be explored. So it just seemed like a very logical thing to develop, and obviously it was. It just took off. It kind of surprised me. It started off with small realistic figures with some Halloween makeup, and one thing just led to another. And the next thing I knew, I had sort of fallen into something.

MENTORS AND ROLE MODELS

Josef Ackermann

CHIEF EXECUTIVE OFFICER, CHAIRMAN, AND DIRECTOR, DEUTSCHE BANK

Josef Ackermann has changed the direction of Deutsche Bank from a generally German bank to an international financial institution. He has done it with quiet diplomacy and strong character. In his advice to us, he recommends that in the face of challenges, distractions, and changes, we use mentors and the act of mentoring others to help us stay focused.

———————

Josef Ackermann serves as CEO of Deutsche Bank AG and has been chairman of its Management Board since February 1, 2006. Before taking over his responsibilities at Deutsche Bank, he worked for Credit Suisse. Ackermann became renowned at Deutsche Bank for shifting the style of management from a conventional mode to one that focused on the needs of shareholders and on international expansion. He has become one of the most powerful men in Germany's financial industry.

STAY FOCUSED

Stay focused on your goals. Learn from criticism, but do not let it distract or slow you down. Look for a mentor who can guide you through decisions and changes and shifts in strategic direction. Be a mentor if you can. Find a career that is in line with your interests, abilities, and work ethic, and success will follow.

Warren M. Washington

SENIOR SCIENTIST, NATIONAL CENTER
FOR ATMOSPHERIC RESEARCH

Science and engineering are his fields, and now he's a senior scientist. With a wealth of knowledge about the equations, formulae, and theories within his fields, Warren M. Washington also has a wealth of knowledge about the *pioneers* within his fields. This knowledge about the great contributors of one's chosen path, Washington explains, can give you models for success.

Warren M. Washington is a senior scientist and head of the Climate Change Research Section in the Climate and Global Dynamics Division at the National Center for Atmospheric Research (NCAR). He held the office of president of the American Meteorological Society (AMS) in 1994 and was past president in 1995. In May 1995 he was appointed by President Clinton to a six-year term on the National Science Board, which helps oversee the National Science Foundation and advises the Executive Branch and Congress on science-related matters. He chaired the Board from 2002 to 2006.

READ ABOUT THE LIVES OF GREAT CONTRIBUTORS

The greatest challenge that I had to overcome was to convince myself that I could become a scientist. There are many great men and women of science, and as a young boy I did not know if that was possible for me. I was greatly helped by reading stories about famous scientists and engineers such as Albert Einstein and George Washington Carver. Reading these stories showed me that many of them came from ordinary families and that they had normal childhoods. Also, many of them had difficult times, sometimes with school. They all showed desire for hard work and at times had to overcome personal challenges.

My suggestion to young people is that not only should they read about the history of science and engineering, but they should read about the lives of those who have made contributions to these fields.

Jürgen Hambrecht

Chairman of one of the world's largest chemical companies, Jürgen Hambrecht is unimposing but inspirational and is reorganizing the company with concern for environmental protection. In his letter Hambrecht emphasizes the important role mentors can play in your growth.

Jürgen Hambrecht is the CEO and member of the Board of Management of BASF. He has been a member of the Supervisory Board of Bilfinger Berger (a construction company) in Mannheim, Germany, since 2000 and has been president of the German Chemical Industry Association since 2003. He became head of Research and Purchasing at Lacke und Farben in Münster, Gemany (now BASF Coatings) in 1985; president of Engineering Plastics Division in 1990; and president of East Asia division based in Hong Kong in 1995. Hambrecht has been a member of the Board of Directors since 1997 and chairman of the Board of Executive Directors of BASF Aktiengesellschaft since May 2003.

SOMEBODY TO HELP

The first thing is that you have to have a vision of your own, and then you need to work hard to become one of the best. You need to be among the best in order to really grow. Sometimes it's difficult to do that on your own. You may need somebody to help and direct you, like a mentor. I always had people with whom I could talk. Sometimes you may run a little bit too fast in one direction, which may not be the right way to go. A mentor can help you be self-critical, which I think is the most important thing. And you need to have both feet on the ground.

Robert Keith Gray

He is probably the world's foremost public relations expert and although retired still counsels a small number of corporations and leaders. As secretary of the Eisenhower Cabinet, Robert Keith Gray established contacts that are still running governments today. Amid the humor of Gray's letter lies great advice to heed the virtues and expectations your parents offer you.

A Cabinet member in the Eisenhower Administration, Robert Keith Gray took Gray & Company public, and later became worldwide chairman of Hill and Knowlton. Gray served as national communications director for the Reagan-Bush campaign and became co-chairman of Reagan's Inaugural Committee. He has an MBA from Harvard and has been awarded four honorary doctorates.

YOUR MOTHER'S EXPECTATIONS

My greatest challenge—the greatest challenge for anyone born in the last century to a Midwest mother—has
been to meet parental expectations.

Farm-state mothers expect you to be honest, upright,
loyal, patriotic; in short, to possess all the good virtues
and to live your life in their demonstration. They take
as a given you will not litter. They know you will search
for the owners of found goods. They expect you to return shopping carts to the mall.

They also assume you will strive to achieve in whatever field you chose. What son of the Midwest did not
hear his mother say, "We expect great things of you"?
And she meant to be taken literally and not to expect
her to be surprised when the big news came.

Italy once flattered me with its highest honor. My
mother, along with some 200 including a former first
lady, attended the ceremony. Others congratulated me
after the ambassador had hung the beribboned medal
around my neck.

My mother's only comment, "I wish the ribbon had been blue." Aspire to meet your mother's expectations. They always will be higher than your own.

Stephen Joel Trachtenberg

PRESIDENT EMERITUS AND UNIVERSITY PROFESSOR OF PUBLIC SERVICE, THE GEORGE WASHINGTON UNIVERSITY

The George Washington University in Washington,
D.C., has more future world leaders going through
its halls and Stephen Joel Trachtenberg's office than
most other schools. His concern for integrity, expressed
here in his letter, even crosses into the courses that
professors teach at his university.

Stephen Joel Trachtenberg served for thirty years as a
university president. He is now president emeritus and
university professor of public service at the George
Washington University, where he teaches courses on the
university presidency in America. He is also an adviser
to Korn/Ferry International, where he is helping to find
the next generation of university leadership. His most
recent book is *Big Man on Campus: A University President
Speaks Out On Higher Education.*

INTEGRITY, BRED IN THE BONE

Any young person who asked me about integrity in business and the role of leadership in the business world would get a two-part answer from me. This may reflect the inescapable intellectual balancing act that goes on at any university and certainly goes on here at the George Washington University. "On the one hand," we say, "but on the other . . ." This is not, I hasten to assure you, a weakness in the American academy, but one of its glories. Simply, there is no panacea, no one way to make everything right.

The first part of my answer about the future of integrity and leadership would be cynical, or at least utterly practical. Look, I would say, just look at what has been going on recently in businesses. Look at the financial shenanigans at Enron and WorldCom and Arthur Andersen—and look at what their behavior has cost them. All of them are wrecked. Look at the behavior of some of the great investment firms, which have had to pay substantial fines. Look, I would finally say, at the parade of civil and criminal suits already brought (and being contemplated) against so many leaders in business. And I would stress *leaders*, because the problems I have enumerated—and they are all quite familiar, even part of our folklore now—were not the work of underlings in most cases, but of leaders.

So my cynical response, if it really is cynical, would be this: Look at what happens when you lack integrity, when your behavior is bad, when your greed overrules your sense of fair play, when your ethical sense grows dull. You can get caught and, aside from ruining your own life and career, look at the damage you can do others. It doesn't pay.

This may not be the most inspiring way to get people to think about integrity and the responsibilities of leadership, but I imagine it is a good way to get their attention. I do not believe there was ever a Golden Age of business, when everybody did the right thing and no one feathered his own nest at a high cost to others, let alone to his own conscience. Bad things have just been more widespread—or maybe just better and more widely reported—in recent years, and I think it is worth taking advantage of this well-known news to instill a sense of shame. This is, I confess, an old-fashioned word, but we often pay at least lip service to old-fashioned virtues and mourn their passing. One of the things that, in my own youthful experience, undergirded old-fashioned virtue was an old-fashioned fear that if I did something wrong and was caught, I'd die of shame and so would my parents.

There is also the second side to the advice I would give, the optimistic side. American business has been the admiration of the world for more than a century. It has produced new products and services, it has created employment, and it has created extraordinary wealth—not just for the biggest stockholders, but for the nation as a whole. Business is a worthy field for the efforts of bright young men and women. It is, moreover, a field that has an endless hunger for leaders because business is constantly expanding—or, in periods of downturn, expects to recover through expansion.

Thus, business needs expansive leaders. But business also needs leaders who appear trustworthy because they *are* trustworthy, leaders who will keep their promises to their employees, stockholders, and customers. To put it simply—and as optimistically as I can—I would say that business needs leaders for whom integrity is built in or second nature, if you will. Integrity is not a product or the result of a course on the way to earning an MBA. It is not a veneer or a public stance. To the contrary, it should be bred in the bone and be as important in one's life as one's public life; always on and functioning, 24/7.

Leaders with such a deep-seated sense of integrity could, I believe, profoundly and rather quickly help restore a great deal of the public's confidence in American business. Good leaders would also choose to work with others who have the same sense of integrity or, failing such perfect recruits, do everything they can to instill the same belief in the irrevocable importance of integrity.

This last point is important: Part of leadership is the ability to teach formally *and* by example. Are there such young people available today? Are they on the campuses of America's colleges and universities? And are they thinking of careers in business and especially hoping for positions of leadership? Yes to all questions. Are there enough of them? I don't know the answer to that. I think it has to be part of any university's mission to look at the character of its students and to encourage them to do the right thing. In other words, to increase the number of young men and women for whom integrity is the norm.

This is no easy job, but neither is teaching quantum physics or neurosurgery, both of which we do extremely well. The questions "leaders" have raised are difficult— and of course that is why they have raised them. But if difficulty were an insurmountable obstacle, there would be no universities—and few if any men and women of any age would be willing to take on the burdens of leadership, no matter how great the rewards. But leading a life of integrity and honesty is not an obstacle but an outlook. And I am, finally, optimistic enough to believe that many young people share that outlook and that many more, seeing their success, will emulate them. Integrity, I would tell them, does pay.

A FINAL NOTE ON *REAL* SUCCESS

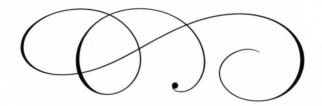

Theodore Forstmann

Theodore Forstmann is a billionaire who has been linked to the most beautiful women in the world, including Princess Diana. He built a major investment firm and now controls one of the largest talent companies in the world, IMG. He is shrewd, extremely intelligent, and, surprisingly for a billionaire, known by many around him as "Mr. Nice Guy." According to Forstmann, you should forget about road maps to achieving financial wealth, because that kind of bounty can be taken away; instead, strive toward wealth of your mind and personality.

Theodore Forstmann is a pioneer of the investment industry, having developed a number of innovative means to deliver superior returns for investors.

Also a committed philanthropist, Forstmann created the Children's Scholarship Fund in 1998, in collaboration with Wal-Mart's John Walton, and has served as a director of the International Rescue Committee.

REAL WEALTH IS NOT PHYSICAL

I teach a lot at different business schools, from Harvard to Stanford to Yale. And business school students always want a map for success. I'm sorry to tell you that if there is a map, I don't know what it is. But I can tell you this: Real wealth is not physical. Real wealth comes in the form of ideas. Physical wealth can disappear; the government can take it away, terrorists can take it away, and so on. Metaphysical wealth cannot be taken away, and it is the driver for all of the growth that takes place in the world. So, when I talk to kids, I say, "Don't ask me how to make a lot of money, because I don't even know." I don't even think that's a particularly worthwhile goal. Instead, be aware of the existence of metaphysical wealth, or in other words, be aware of your own thought process. Be true to yourself, because you don't have anything in the world but yourself. Lose yourself, and you'll have nothing.

ACKNOWLEDGMENTS

The dictionary says that *appreciation* is "the act of estimating the qualities of people and things"—it's gratefulness and gratitude.

And I have a lot to be grateful for and a lot of people to appreciate.

I've never known one person to write a book alone. There are editors, copy editors, publishers, secretaries, assistants, colleagues, and also wives and children who have suggestions.

So as I age, I want to give a thank you to the following, all of whom deserve very much credit. And if they're happy with this mention, I'm available for lunch.

At *LEADERS* magazine: Darrell Brown, our vice chairman who searched our archives for gems; David Schner, our president, who organized and gathered the best of what we printed; and Gerard Cobleigh, our vice president and general manager, who made sure what everyone did was correct, as perfect as possible, and filled with spirit.

At our publisher: Scott Watrous, Gary Krebs, Inger Forland, Michelle Lewy, and especially Keith Wallman, who is one of the nicest people to work with. All of them are delightful people to know. They are a special breed. Georgiana Goodwin's design for the book exudes class and elegance.

Then at Abrams Artists Agency there is a human dynamo named Maura Teitelbaum who arranged this publishing venture, and her boss, Harry Abrams, a sage as well.

Last I give a lot of hugs and kisses to Alice, my wife of fifty-one years; our children, Kaari and Kristi; and our grandchildren, Chelsea and Liliane. They are the ones who keep this old heart pumping.

INDEX

About the Author

Henry O. Dormann, in addition to his position with *LEADERS* magazine, is the editor of *The Speaker's Book of Quotations*. Among his own numerous leadership roles, he was founder and the first executive director of the Library of Presidential Papers (now the Center for the Study of the Presidency), and served as president of the United States Technical Developments Company, a division of U.S. Banknote Corporation. He divides his time between Bath, New York, and New York City.

Warren M. Washington